THE CRAFT OF REVISION

THIRD EDITION

THE CRAFT OF REVISION
THIRD EDITION

DONALD M. MURRAY

HARCOURT BRACE COLLEGE PUBLISHERS

FORT WORTH PHILADELPHIA SAN DIEGO NEW YORK ORLANDO AUSTIN SAN ANTONIO
TORONTO MONTREAL LONDON SYDNEY TOKYO

Publisher	Christopher P. Klein
Executive Editor	Michael Rosenberg
Product Manager	Ilse Wolfe West
Developmental Editor	Laurie Runion
Project Editor	Mary K. Mayo
Art Director	Linda Wooton
Production Manager	Kathleen Ferguson

Cover Image: © 1997 by Pierre-Yves Goavec

ISBN: 0-15-505446-5

Library of Congress Catalog Card Number: 97-70009

Address for Editorial Correspondence: Harcourt Brace College Publishers, 301 Commerce Street, Suite 3700, Fort Worth, TX 76102.

Address for Orders: Harcourt Brace & Company, 6277 Sea Harbor Drive, Orlando, FL 32887-6777. 1-800-782-4479.

Website address: http://www.hbcollege.com

Harcourt Brace & Company will provide supplements or supplement packages to those adopters qualified under our adoption policy. Please contact your sales representative to learn how you qualify. If as an adopter or potential user you receive supplements you do not need, please return them to your sales representative or send them to: Attn: Returns Department, Troy Warehouse, 465 South Lincoln Drive, Troy, MO 63379.

Printed in the United States of America

8 9 0 1 2 3 4 5 6 016 10 9 8 7 6 5 4 3

....

for Minnie Mae
Who made soup of old bones
and mailed out manuscripts
in which I had no faith

....

OTHER TEXTBOOKS BY
DONALD M. MURRAY

Write to Learn, fifth edition (Harcourt Brace, 1996)

Crafting a Life in Essay, Story, Poem (Heinemann, 1996)

Writer in the Newsroom (Poynter Institute for Media Studies, 1996)

Read to Write, third edition (Harcourt Brace, 1993)

Writing for Your Readers, second edition (Globe Pequot Press, 1992)

Shoptalk: Learning to Write with Writers (Heinemann, Boynton/ Cook, 1990)

Expecting the Unexpected (Heinemann, Boynton/Cook, 1989)

Learning by Teaching, second edition (Heinemann, Boynton/Cook, 1989)

A Writer Teaches Writing, second edition (Houghton Mifflin, 1985)

PREFACE

I've been messing around with *The Craft of Revision*—again. No surprise that a writer fascinated with the process of revision should keep playing his textbooks toward new understandings. The game of revision is not superficial. As Ernest Hemingway said, "Prose is architecture, not interior decoration." In revision—reseeing what we have written—we see what we may begin to write.

I have reread each line of the second edition to discover the third edition, changing a word, a phrase, a sentence, a paragraph, a page—cutting, adding, moving around—to understand the process of revision more clearly and to share that new clarity with students.

I have saved the basic process of revision but renamed part of the process to reflect more accurately what the rewriting writer is doing:

Rewrite to Focus
Rewrite to Collect
Rewrite for External Order [Formerly, to Shape]
Rewrite for Internal Order [Formerly, to Order]
Rewrite to Develop
Rewrite with Voice
Rewrite to Edit

I have cut the second and third chapters of the previous edition, saving the best parts and integrating them elsewhere in the book so the student gets to the revision process more quickly.

I have also broken down the chapter on order in response to students' difficulties with order. One chapter deals with the question of form and genre—external order—and the other with logic, sequence, pace, and emphasis—internal order.

CASE HISTORIES AND INTERVIEWS

We have retained two case histories and added a new one that discusses the search for an appropriate voice. We have also added interviews with three professional writers and three students that each focus on the rewriting task identified in a particular chapter. These practicing writers describe the attitudes and techniques they use to solve their revision and editing problems.

EXERCISES

Students are invited to perform specific writing tasks within the book. These exercises are woven into the book so the student may use them in the context of a specific rewriting problem, either on their own or at their instructor's suggestion. More than classroom activities, the exercises are techniques any writer—student or professional—may find helpful when facing a writing problem.

WHO CAN USE THIS TEXT?

We have been astonished, and delighted, at how *The Craft of Revision* has been used in diverse learning environments. It has been adopted for first-year English courses in universities and community colleges and has also been popular in advanced composition programs.

The Craft of Revision has been used in middle and high school classrooms, in college remedial and honors programs, in graduate seminars, and in teacher training courses and workshops. It has been adopted by corporate and governmental training programs. It has been studied by the writing staffs of newspapers and as a supplemental text in creative writing courses. And it has been used by individuals who are teaching themselves to write.

REVISION AT WORK

The third edition closes with an extensive new chapter that shows revision at work in school and on the job after graduation. It provides examples of many forms of writing and offers specific guidelines for revising each one that the student can use during the course and afterward in other classes and in the workplace.

HOW CAN STUDENTS LEARN THE CRAFT OF REVISION?

Students, first of all, must learn a positive attitude toward revision. The process of revision, for most students, has not been concerned with finding meaning, but it has focused on editing superficial mechanical and grammatical errors to a preconceived and often not clearly understood standard. It is important that students see revision in a larger context which includes editing, but is not only a matter of editing.

Here are some ways this positive attitude can be reinforced in the composition class:

- First readings by the student writer, the instructor, and classmates should focus on potential, not error.
- There should be time for revision, which usually means fewer papers, revised more extensively.
- The best as well as the worst papers should have the benefits of revision.
- Students should observe the discoveries of meaning made clear by revision on classmates' papers as well as on their own.
- The process of revision should be sequential, moving from a concern with meaning through audience, form, information, structure, to language.

Above all, attitude motivates the learning of skills. The instructor should reinforce a constructive attitude toward revision. Some of the ways this can be done:

- Share evolving drafts that document the positive results of revision. Reveal the instructor's own revision case histories, have students who have revised effectively share their own case histories, share the case histories of successful revision from interviews and biographies of writers.
- Ask class members and possibly faculty members from other disciplines to report on activities in their disciplines that are similar to revision: play and musical rehearsal, practice in a sport, the process of painting, experiments in science.
- Have the class perform quick revisions. For example, write a five-line description of a familiar place or person in five minutes, then do five-minute rewrites from a different point of view, for a different purpose, for a different audience, in a different form, in a different voice, and share the results so the class appreciates the different, diverse products of revision.

At each stage of the revision process students should play with the skills of shifting focus, appealing to different audiences, experimenting with form, manipulating information, restructuring, tuning the draft's voice.

SIX WAYS TO USE *THE CRAFT OF REVISION* IN YOUR CLASSROOM

This textbook has been designed to support the student and instructor in many different courses. It can be used alone or as a supplement to other rhetorics and readers. Teachers will and should find their own different ways to adapt *The Craft of Revision* to their particular teaching style, the needs of their own students, or to the curriculum in which they function. These suggestions are designed to spark the diversity that should be central to teaching writing.

1. *The Craft of Revision,* third edition, can be used as the principal writing text because it helps students create a first draft. The students can use it to help them write weekly papers or to support a sequence of three-week units in which they write a draft and perform two major revisions supported by conferences, peer workshops, and class instruction sessions. I have had good results with students working on one paper all semester, taking several weeks to find the subject and then moving week by week through the revision process. No, they didn't get bored, since they found subjects they wanted to explore. In fact, alumni response has been unusually strong, saying they really learned to write when they had time to learn the craft of revision.

2. *The Craft of Revision* can supplement a rhetoric that has limited material on revision, or it can supplement a reader, allowing the student to understand the craft that created the models and to practice the same craft on their own drafts.

3. *The Craft of Revision* can be introduced to the class the first week or two and then used as a desk book by the students as they revise their papers. The best way to do this is to have the students write a paragraph in class, then revise it a number of times, sharing each revision with a small group that will select the most interesting leap toward meaning to share with the whole class.

   The students may need to be told, in the beginning, what to do, since they have only been told to edit in the past. I usually say, "Develop the potential in your draft, exploring the subject in writing any way you want, but if you're stuck you may want to change the point of view from which the subject is seen."

   Some other suggestions I may make are to try to make the information more specific, revise it for a different publication or audience, write with more emotion or less, try to write in a different voice.

   The writing periods should be short, no more than five minutes, and the peer sharing session should be no longer than fifteen minutes. It always helps if the instructor performs the same exercise and shares those drafts. Once the students experience the discovery that is possible with revision, they can be introduced to the text.

4. *The Craft of Revision* may be used in the latter half of a composition semester or term when the students have drafts worthy of careful revision and when they see the need for revision.

5. *The Craft of Revision* may be used in a content course in English or any other discipline to help the students improve their writing assignments. The text may be assigned to all students in the course or suggested as an aid to those students who are having difficulty revising effectively.

6. *The Craft of Revision* can be used as a self-teaching text with the student creating a draft and moving through the sequential steps to practice the skills of revision.

In every case the students should use the textbook in connection with their own writing. The craft of revision cannot be learned in the abstract; theory must be illuminated by practice that will, in turn, illuminate theory.

However the textbook is used, it will help the individual student, the instructor, and the whole class if those students who do an effective job of revision testify to the class on what they did and how, which will reinforce the student and instruct everyone else. I have done this with oral reports but more recently with quickly written but complete commentaries that the students write, reporting on their writing and revision process, their writing problems, and their proposed solutions. These commentaries encourage tudents to examine their craft and teach them how they can identify and solve their own writing problems. Those solutions instruct us all.

My students have always instructed me, and I have told worried beginning writing teachers to get their students writing. In every class, some students write better than others. Get them to tell you and the class how they write, and the curriculum will evolve.

....

ACKNOWLEDGMENTS

Laurie Runion, one of the very best editors with whom I have ever worked, has made significant contributions to the design of the edition and to each page. Michael Rosenberg saved the first edition from total failure. Without him there would have been no second or third editions.

My wife, Minnie Mae, is my first reader and most demanding critic. Chip Scanlan, my closest friend, who is director of writing programs at The Poynter Institute for Media Studies in St. Petersburg, Florida, is always as close as the telephone.

Brock Dethier, Thomas Newkirk, Donald Graves, and many other colleagues in the writing community at the University of New Hampshire have contributed to my continuing education. Others who have stimulated my thinking and influenced this book include Bonnie Sunstein of the University of Iowa, Thomas Romano of Miami University in Ohio, Driek Zirinsky of Boise State University, Lad Tobin of Boston College, and the writer Ralph Fletcher.

Mary Clark of the English Department at the University of New Hampshire is an expert linguist and a fine teacher. She made important contributions to the first edition and her mark remains on this edition.

I am indebted to the professionalism of Mary Mayo, project editor; Anne Lesser, copyeditor; Linda Wooton, designer; and Kathy Ferguson, production manager.

The reviewers who helped me with their candid and insightful comments on this edition are Sally Harvey, Yuba College; Elizabeth Hodges, Virginia Commonwealth University; Ingrid Jordak, Broome Community College at Binghamton; and Donna Qualley, Western Washington University.

I was also instructed by the honest, detailed responses of those who reviewed the first and second editions: Kay Baker, Ricks College; Kathleen Bell, Old Dominion University; Mary Comstock, University of Puget Sound; Marie Czarnecki, Mohawk Valley Community College; Francine DeFrance, Cerritos College; Connie Hale, University of Puget Sound; Dick Harrington, Piedmont Virginia

Community College; Pat Huyett, University of Missouri at Kansas City; Ernest Lee, Carson-Newman College; Joan Tyler Mead, Marshall University; Leslie Prast, Delta College; David Roberts, Samford University; Susan Roberts, Boston College; Bernard Selzler, University of Minnesota at Crookston; Nancy Walker, Southwest Missouri State University; and Driek Zirinsky, Boise State University.

For what works, all just listed and many more should take credit; for what does not work, the author accepts the blame.

CONTENTS

....

CHAPTER 3
REWRITE TO COLLECT 47

....

CHAPTER 4
REWRITE FOR EXTERNAL
ORDER 76

....

CHAPTER 5
REWRITE FOR INTERNAL
ORDER 104

CHAPTER 6
REWRITE TO DEVELOP   118

CHAPTER 7
REWRITE WITH VOICE   151

CHAPTER 8
REWRITE TO EDIT   170

....

CHAPTER 9
REWRITE AT WORK   204

....

CHAPTER 10
THE CRAFT OF LETTING GO   229

....

CHAPTER 1

WRITE TO REWRITE

Do you ever write badly?

Good. All writers write badly—at first. Nobel Prize winners, Pulitzer Prize winners, writers of blockbuster movies, writers with distinguished academic reputations, writers who influence and persuade, instruct and inspire, comfort and anger and amuse and inform, they all write badly. Writers who write novels, speeches, news stories, screenplays, corporate memos, textbooks, plays, poems, history books, scientific reports, legal briefs, grant applications, TV scripts, songs all write badly—at first.

Then they rewrite. Revision is not the end of the writing process but the beginning. First emptiness, then terror, at last one word, then a few words, a paragraph, a page, finally a draft that can be revised.

WHY DO WE FEAR REWRITING?

When we revise we do not so much revise the page as revise our thinking, our feeling, our memory, ourselves—who we are. The words we revise stand for something. They are not blanks checks but stand for what we think and what we believe and what we care about and how we see the world.

It is normal for us to fear change, but we should celebrate it. Revision gives us a second chance at life. In fact, it gives us many more chances so we can keep revising—understanding—our childhood, the war, the writing process, aging, the territories I most explore with writing. Each time we revise we may:

- *Discover that we know more than we thought.* We don't think we remember much about our first trip away from home alone, but as we revise what we have written more and more information comes to mind—and to screen.
- *Change what we think of what we know.* The bad moments on the trip may become instructive as we rewrite.
- *Change what we feel about what we know.* The trip we thought was a disaster becomes humorous in the revised draft.
- *Extend what we know as the draft makes unexpected connections.* The writer may see, for example, that the trip alone three years ago prepared the writer for college or military service.
- *Move the point of view from which we view the subject.* The first draft may have described the trip as it took place, and now we look back from the experiences of many trips away from home and put it in a new perspective.

Most of us are not trained to revise. Our parents, relatives, neighbors, friends, religious leaders, schools, employers urge us to believe, not doubt; accept, not change; obey, not question. If we revise our lives we may, of course, unbalance the relationships we have with family, lovers, friends, colleagues. It appears more comfortable to live the unexamined life.

But it is not. The world in which we live changes. We must revise our lives to incorporate what is new with what we know and believe. We must revise to survive.

Do *not* think revision is superficial. Revision is the reordering of experience so that it reveals meaning. It is the great adventure of the mind.

HOW DO I FIND SOMETHING TO WRITE ABOUT?

I interview myself to discover what I need to explore by writing. The interview always makes my world expand. My life that seemed dull and ordinary becomes more interesting as I listen to the answers to my own questions. The same thing may happen to you if you answer my questions.

- What am I thinking about when I'm waiting for somebody? What irritated me today? What made me laugh? What made me angry? What did I learn today?
- What contradicted what I know—or thought I knew?
- What made me feel good?
- What made me feel bad?
- What confuses me?
- What does somebody else need to know that I know?
- What questions do I need answered?
- What surprised me today?

 Write down your fragmentary answers as I do. Don't worry about spelling or grammar or neatness or sentences. You are trying to catch an idea, a half of an idea, a quarter of an idea, just the quick glint of where an idea was a moment ago. Play with words, images, facts. See if any of them connect. Pay close attention to anything that surprises you, that is different from what you expected. Follow surprise or connection in your mind or on paper to see where your thinking may take you.

FIND THE INSTIGATING LINE OR IMAGE

Inexperienced writers believe that writing begins with an inflated idea of a vague, general topic such as "truth," "beauty," or "patriotism" because they have been given such assignments in school. What they don't know is that published writers would do as badly as they do with such assignments unless they can come up with an instigating line or an image that is specific and, above all, interesting to them.

An instigating line is a fragment of language, a sentence or less, that I hear in my mind or find myself scribbling in my notebook. It's the line that contains a tension, contradiction, question, feeling, or thought that surprises me and would be productive to think more about in writing.

Let's take those vague topics I just mentioned and see what would happen if we had an instigating line to start us writing:

• "TRUTH" •

"My first football coach was a Catholic priest—taught us how to lie—to fake injuries."

The conflict between the religious practice and football practice interests me. In church we were instructed to tell the truth and on the playing field we practiced fake injuries that would give us a time-out we didn't deserve—and an unfair advantage over the other team.

I gave a lecture at a college whose football team was called the Fighting Quakers, a good example of an instigating line as we imagine a group of hard-hitting pacifists. There are many essays in exploring the messages given by sports that contradict other social messages such as "don't fight," "winning isn't everything," "violence is bad."

• "BEAUTY" •

"Told mother I was fat, guys made jokes about me. She had same thing happen at same school—she was too thin, no 'sweater' girl. She weighed same as I weigh."

This observation presents a conflict that needs exploration. Women are shaped by nature and so are men. *Fat* and *thin* are relative terms. So is *beauty.* Look at the pictures of film stars years ago. How dangerous it is to allow society to define you. How many are hurt who are not considered beautiful? How many are hurt by being considered beautiful or handsome and not taken seriously as a student? Those are a few of the topics that might grow from one line.

• "PATRIOTISM" •

"Spies are traitorous patriots."

A fascinating and thoughtful essay for a course in history, ethics, or political science could grow out of this fragmentary idea. Graham Greene once asked, "Isn't disloyalty as much the writer's virtue as loyalty is the soldier's?" Good question. Is the role of artists to stand apart from society and take stock? What about priests who criticize the Vatican, senators who vote against their party, soldiers who oppose a particular war? And what is a patriot anyway? Irish men and women are patriots in Ireland and traitors in Northern Ireland—and the other way around. All these are good pieces that could be researched and written.

Writers also find writing can begin with an image, a mind picture that itches the imagination, that makes you look at it again and again to see what it means. All of us have images that haunt us. I remember seeing my face when I was a baby reflected in the glass of a china cabinet and that became a poem. I remember the long, empty corridors of high school between classes, so different from the way I usually saw them crowded with students. When I found why I remembered them—why I was so often alone in the corridor—I found an essay.

When I am given an assignment to write an academic paper, I do the same thing I do when searching for a poem. I sit with pen in hand and notebook open or without anything but my own thoughts. Sometimes I think about what I think about when I am not thinking: when I'm waiting for class to begin, sitting in a car waiting for someone, when my mind drifts away from the people to whom I should be listening, during the commercials on television, when I'm walking alone, just before I drop off to sleep. At these times, an image, a word, a fragment of language will pass through the black emptiness like a shooting star. I capture it in a scribbled note.

Other times I listen to what I'm saying when I talk to myself, or I remember what has surprised me recently. What did I see, think, feel,

hear, watch, read that was not expected—in fact that ran against expectations, shocking or confusing me—contradicting what I thought
I had known or believed?

Many people believe writing comes to the writer like a computer
printout, flowing along, finished, complete. Writing usually comes in
fragments—details, hints, clues, collisions of information, half ideas
and quarter ideas, bits of pieces of information, scraps that have fallen
out of books, from TV or radio, from conversations at the next table
or in another room. The writer plays with these scraps to see what
they may mean.

I start listing in a notebook or on a computer what passes
through my unthinking mind. This technique, called *brainstorming*,
is a method of extracting from memory what you don't know you
remember, what you have forgotten, or what you were never aware
you observed, and allowing these pieces of information to rub
against one another. Brainstorming works with ideas as well as
memory, or with information collected for an academic paper.

To brainstorm, put aside all your notes, take a piece of paper,
and put down whatever occurs to you in a fragmentary list. Surprise
yourself. Be silly, dumb, an enemy to your own preconceived ideas.
You can work by yourself or with a team. Brainstorming is ideal
when a committee is planning a party, a marketing campaign, a new
research project. Work fast, with as little conscious thought as possible. When you are done, circle the items that surprised you the most,
and draw arrows between items that have some connection. This
should produce an instigating line.

I begin by just thinking about a time in my life—high school—
and start brainstorming:

> The principal, Mr. Collins
>
> North Quincy High
>
> Long prison corridors, lockers, students locked in cells—class-
> rooms
>
> Round glasses on round face
>
> Can't see his eyes
>
> Cold oak bench outside principal's office

Detention

Boring

Not in school when in school

Working in meat market

Sitting in class, eyes open, asleep

CIRCLE THE LINE OR IMAGE THAT SURPRISES

I suspend my critical judgment, not looking for good writing, but simply a word, a phrase, an image, a hint of an idea, two items or three that connect or are in conflict: whatever surprises or interests me. Surprise is the most productive reaction for me; I like to discover I have written something that itches, something I would not have predicted I would have put on my list.

The surprise doesn't have to be a history-shattering idea, just something I hadn't thought about, not in that way anyway. I look at one item on my list—"not in school when in school"—and ask myself what that means. I slept and ate, mostly, at home, and I attended school at least four days a week. But I lived on the street. The gang on the street corner was the family that counted most. My real and imagined lives were at work and on the street, not in my apartment or in my classrooms. No surprise there. I cut school a lot—every Thursday my senior year—and dropped out twice. No surprise to me in that. I have written that story before. But I had never faced up to the fact that I was "not in school when in school."

Looking back, that interests me. I don't know if I have anything to say, but I may. Writing may tell me. That phrase, "not in school when in school," is a small surprise, but it sparks questions: Where was I? What did I find there that I didn't find in school? How did I manage to be in two places at once? And "sitting in class, eyes open, asleep." Well, that's one form of escape. How did I do that?

EXPLORE THE SURPRISING LINE OR IMAGE

But I don't start writing yet. I make another list focusing on the item or items I've chosen to explore—"sitting, eyes open, asleep"; "not in school when in school"—and again list anything that comes into my mind connected to what I am exploring. I scribble specific details, statistics, facts, memories, observations, feelings, fragmentary thoughts, not in sentences but in words and small chunks of language.

marching asleep in the army
looking awake but sleeping in faculty meetings
during commercials
at family dinners
escaping into fantasy
    memory
    stories I tell myself
    other places
    other people—"empathy"
protection against bores
    against boring sermons
    classes
    jobs
how I look as if I'm listening when I'm not
how can I tell someone else is not listening to me when they look as if they are

HOW DO I CREATE A DISCOVERY DRAFT?

Now it is time to explore the subject further in a first or rough draft that I call a *discovery draft*. Once more, I do not write what I already know or what I expect to say, but I write what I do not know. I am thinking in writing, the most disciplined form of thought. And I find it fun because I keep finding I know more than I expected, feel more than I expected, remember more and have a stronger opinion than I expected.

WRITE WITH VELOCITY

I write as fast as I can because velocity is as important in writing a discovery draft as it is in riding a bicycle. You have to get up to speed to get anywhere. My handwriting and my typing are appallingly bad. It is hard to read what I've written at top speed but I must write with velocity to outrace the censor or to fail.

Outrace the Censor

All of us have the well intentioned—parents, teachers, editors, the critical self—who censor what we say. It is important to write as fast as possible to escape them, not worrying about making sense or following the rules of language so we can discover what has been hidden in our minds.

Fail

Failure is essential to effective writing. It is the failure that instructs the chemist, the football coach, the defense attorney, the entrepreneur, the writer. An attempt is made. It doesn't work. But the way it fails instructs. Robyn Davidson, the travel writer who has written about traveling with nomads in *Desert Places,* said, "Thank God for being a writer. Because you do sort of find out what you think by the process of writing." Davidson goes on, "The French word for wanderlust or wandering is 'errance.' The etymology is the same as 'error.' So to wander is to make mistakes. In other words, to make mistakes, to make errors is a sort of the idea of learning through trial and error, allowing the mistakes to be part of the process."

I have a hint of an idea. I am surprised at the contradictory feelings I have when I begin to learn a new computer program. I write:

> My feelings are complex and contradictory as I learn a new computer program.

That is a failed sentence, grammatically correct but bland and without a full load of meaning. I try to write it to discover what I mean and use specifics that will make it less bland, more interesting. I rewrite:

> I am unlearning WordPerfect and learning Word a keystroke at a time. Click. My formatting toolbar is a box in the middle of my document. I try View and Tools and Format, sinking further

and further into despair. Then I try dragging the box up to where it belongs. It works. I am ecstatic. I am a problem solver. I have experienced fear and success, and I realize that I am motivated to learn by the exciting contradictory feelings of terror and joy.

The first sentence gave me the instruction I needed to write the later sentences.

WRITE OUT LOUD

The Spanish Nobel Prize–winning novelist, Camilo Tose Cela, says, ". . . when I write I do it aloud. Many faults and cacophonies that the ear is able to catch cannot be seen on the written page. So, if it sounds poorly to my ear I can catch the error. Sometimes it takes me quite a long time to discover what isn't working, that a word is lacking or that one needs to be taken out, but I insist on searching for it and finally finding what's wrong; that there is a word missing or that a comma isn't placed correctly, etc. It comes from listening."

We learned to speak before we wrote, and, even if we are writers, we speak thousands upon thousands of words more than we write in a day. When we write, we speak in written words. The magic of writing is that readers who may never meet us, hear what we have written. Music rises from the page when we read.

We call the heard quality of writing *voice,* and it may be the most important element in writing. Voice, like background music in a movie, is tuned to the writing, supports and extends what the writing says. Listen to master writers speak of voice:

> *Imagine yourself at your kitchen table, in your pajamas. Imagine one person you'd allow to see you that way, and write in the voice you'd use to that friend.* SANDRA CISNEROS, NOVELIST.
>
> *I read everything that I write aloud. First, the paragraph. Then, the page. Then, the chapter. And finally, I read the whole book aloud. Because I want to hear my voice reading it, and I need it to sound natural.* ISABEL ALLENDE, JOURNALIST AND NOVELIST.
>
> *I hear a thousand "voices" in my head. They are the voices of my characters. They are male, female, white, brown and yellow.* BHARATI MUKHERJEE, NOVELIST.

The longer you stay a writer, the more voices you find in your own voice and the more voices you find in the world. ALLAN GURGANUS, NOVELIST.

But voice serves the writer before the reader. It is the voice of the writing that tells the writer the potential meaning of what is written in a discovery draft, reveals its emotional intensity, its importance to the writer and to readers. A college freshman might write:

> My first weekend I expected everything to be the same as I left. The house had shrunk, the driveway was shorter than I remembered. The yard was smaller and my room had become a sewing room. My girlfriend had become a friend, a distant friend who asked me for advice about some Elmer. I gave it. As if I was some university stud, not a guy who hadn't even walked to class with a girl yet. My old friends were gone and my folks treated me like company. I was a stranger to my life and I liked it. I wasn't that kid who lived in my room. Mother came home early from the real estate office and we just talked as if I were her son's friend home from college. When Dad came home we had a beer and we went out to dinner with Uncle Val and my latest aunt. They treated me as if I were grown-up, dirty jokes and everything, and perhaps I was, perhaps my folks and I were friends.

I hear an individual voice, the voice of a person I'd like to know, someone who experiences the unexpected and makes something of it. I like the music of *"The house had shrunk, the driveway was shorter than I remembered," "some Elmer,"* and *"I was a stranger to my life and I liked it."* I suspect that voice has not yet been heard by the writer, but it should be. That draft needs to be developed, but it is a good first draft: a voice can be heard in a tailgating car wreck of language.

In the next draft, a student assigned to write a paper on the British essayist George Orwell's "The Hanging" wrote a rough discovery draft that begins like this:

> I didn't like being assigned the Orwell essay in freshman English. I felt the instructor was messing with my head. My father is a sheriff and we believe in capital punishment and this is an English class and not political science or Liberal 1. But I had to write a critical paper and read the essay one more time. It seemed to be about

standing by and not doing anything like when Joe was being made fun of. I didn't join in but I didn't make friends either. After his suicide we tried to understand, I tried to, if there was anything I—we—could have done. I remembered seeing what was happening, not knowing what would happen of course, at a distance. Orwell knew what was happening but he was a colonial officer, part of the system, and so was I, I suppose, so was I. Standing, watching, doing nothing. That coldness was scary and I guess, it was doing this English paper, that I see how Orwell did that, too.

The student has surprised herself by her second reading, by the connection with an incident in high school, and by her voice that recreates her guilt at her distance and possibly her sin of omission or her sin of passive participation. Now she has an idea for her paper and can read the essay documenting the techniques Orwell used to reveal distance.

You should—as these students did—draft your papers out loud, listening to what your voice is saying, using all your experience with speaking and listening to language, tuning that voice during revision toward a piece of writing that will be heard by readers. Voice is so central that it has its own chapter (Chapter 7) with a case history on how I, as a writer, listen for a voice, then tune it. You don't have to wait until you get to Chapter 7 to read it. Browse through it now if you want to learn more about voice.

WHAT HAPPENS IF I DISCOVER NOTHING IN MY DISCOVERY DRAFT?

You have discovered *something* even if the discovery draft didn't work for you this time. When this happens, you have several choices. Try them:

1. Take a break, then return to the discovery draft and read it again, almost casually, as if it had been written by a stranger. When my mind wanders off in an interesting way, I note the wandering that may become my topic and go back to what caused it.

2. Do a new discovery draft. Of course it doesn't work every time. But take another run at it; see where the flow of language carries you this time.

3. Try other techniques such as brainstorming to see if they work. It is hard for some students to write a discovery draft. They can't let themselves go, and that's all right. They have a strong sense of form or language that inhibits discovery by free-flow writing. Fine. Not everyone of us thinks the same way or writes the same way.

DOES MY WRITING HAVE TO BE SO PERSONAL?

A student from a university in the West e-mailed me a response to one of my textbooks that said, in part,

> I have the god-awful experience of being saddled with your book. I am trying to figure out what I find more offensive: either the silly, New Age tone you give in your advice (Tune into the page, dude!) or the fact that you include so much of yourself and what works for you in your book. I want to learn how to write better. Period. I don't really care about your wife (Minnie Mae) and her award-winning bread dough kneading techniques. I don't think that you should tell your war stories, reveal your most personal feelings about your daughter's death (my condolences, by the way), or discuss the ambiguities that you are dealing with from your disturbing childhood.

Of course, I felt the student's comment was an attack the first time I read it on my screen—and it was—but it reveals a common reaction to personal writing. You do not have to be confessional, you do not have to expose experiences and thoughts and feelings you do not want to reveal. But most effective writing, writing that readers read, save, share with others, is autobiographical.

Writing speaks to the human condition. I am uncomfortable when I am driven to write about my daughter's death, but when we went back to Massachusetts General Hospital for a debriefing after her death, the doctor in charge said I must write about it, and my family agreed. I worried, however, that I was in some way exploiting her dying. When an English professor charged me with that in front of an audience, I remembered how many readers had said that sharing my grief in some way comforted them, that I had articulated their feelings, and I knew I had to speak. I have to witness, in the Baptist terms of my youth, about war, marriage, writing, aging, the human fears and joys we all share.

In another sense, the writing we do that seems most detached— the scientific paper, historical essay, social worker report, legal brief, corporate memo, scholarly essay—is all formed by the experience we have had with the topic. All writing is autobiographical. We write what we know or, as short story writer and novelist Grace Paley says, "We write about what we don't know about what we know." Writing is all rooted in personal experience.

Academic scholars have been studying so long that they can write personal experience papers about their research. Of course, they do not look like personal experience papers. They are written in the language and conventions of their discipline in forms appropriate to publication in specialist journals. It is the task of each discipline to train students in its discourse rules, but the skill of writing is usually taught, at the beginning, through personal experience that can draw on what the students know from firsthand observation, discussion at home and in the street, reading, television, listening to the radio, and private reflection.

Academic writing, writing from the outside in, is just as important as personal writing, writing from the inside out, in helping the writer to understand the changing world in which we all live. Writing demonstrates the discipline of the mind; it reveals how the writer assembles evidence into meaning and then develops, by critical thinking, the significance of that meaning. And writing presents the reader with a logical, documented trail of thought that the reader can, in turn, read critically and evaluate.

....

HOW DO I MAKE AN INSTRUCTOR'S IDEA MY OWN?

I started this chapter by demonstrating how to find an idea for a personal experience paper because there is a close relationship between the words *author* and *authority.* The most effective writing takes place when the writer explores a territory with which he or she is familiar.

The writer should be the authority on the subject matter, but the reality of school is that we are tested by writing exams and papers in response to a teacher's assignment. And this will continue after graduation. Our world is becoming more complex and more distant. There are Japanese factories in the United States and U.S.-owned factories in China. Corporations and government agencies depend on written reports sent by mail, modem, and fax machine. And the topics of most of these reports are not initiated by the writer. We will have topics assigned in class and beyond: in the government agency, the corporation, the laboratory, the courtroom.

UNDERSTAND THE ASSIGNMENT

If the assignment is written, read it carefully, marking the important points so you know what you are expected to do and how you are expected to do it. If the assignment is oral, take notes and go over them carefully. Ask questions. It is better to appear unsure now than later. Bad writing is often the direct product of a misunderstood assignment. Good writing on the wrong topic or in an unacceptable form is still a flunk.

INTERVIEW THE ASSIGNMENT

What is the central question to answer or the central problem to be solved? That central issue may be stated explicitly: "Explain the relationship between tax incentives and productivity growth in the automobile industry in the United States and Japan." Or it may be implicit: "Discuss the role of government in international trade."

Put an assignment from another course beside these pages and use it to put my suggestions in the context of your academic life. What assumptions underlie the assignment? The instructor may have assumptions that are so central to the way she looks at the world, that she may think it is not necessary to mention them. Ask the instructor for them, speak to students who are majoring in the subject, or role-play the instructor and imagine what is required. In a research course in psychology or zoology, a paper probably has to have the research method described as well as the results; in a history course, the instructor will expect whatever is discussed to be placed in an accurate historical context; in a literature course, the instructor does not need to have the plot retold but the work evaluated by a critical theory.

And what documentation or evidence does the assignment giver expect? Does the assignment giver want statistics, firsthand observation, case histories, scholarly citations, or some combination of supporting information? What are the traditions of length, form, and style the assignment giver expects? Is the assignment giver impressed with length or brevity? Is the assignment, in part, a test to see whether you can write a literary analysis using the Modern Language Association (MLA) method of citation, a sociological case history, or a chemistry laboratory report?

PUT YOUR PAPER IN THE CONTEXT OF THE COURSE

Each course, corporation, or government agency has its own intellectual environment. Never forget that in writing you are either an apprentice or a practicing historian, psychologist, environmental planner, biologist, business manager. Each discipline has its own climate, its own expectations in written material. A writer, to be effective, needs to know the limitations of the assignment and then discover how to be creative within those limitations. Every art—the business letter, the poem, the research grant—is created from the tension between freedom and discipline.

CONNECT THE ASSIGNMENT WITH WHAT YOU KNOW

The effective assignment writer has performed the reading and the research demanded by the assignment, taken notes that can be read, and has sources documented. Now the creative assignment writer has to think: to find a meaning, a pattern, a significance in the information the writer has collected. Often the best way to do this is to connect the topic with your own experience. You may want to describe your personal experience with divorce in documenting a paper in sociology. More often, however, your personal experience will lead you toward research questions that need answers, and you will use your autobiographical details backstage in developing a paper that is written with the objective distance appropriate to the assignment.

Your perceptions, observations, and conclusions will be influenced by your personal experience—and should be. Even a paper on tax incentives might show how your father's small-town insurance agency shifted to computers and therefore contributed to the national economy because he is receiving small business tax incentives for making the change. He profited, and others profited as well, because of a federal tax law. And the more specific he will allow you to be about what he spent and what he saved in taxes over the next five years, the more credibility your opinion will have with the reader. You will write with more authority if you make intellectual use of experiences that may have been emotional when they occurred.

HOW TO GET THE WRITING DONE: TRICKS OF THE WRITER'S TRADE

Once more I take instruction from Camilo Tose Cela, the Spanish Nobel laureate:

> Picasso once said, "I don't know if inspiration exists, but when it comes, it usually finds me working." One time a woman asked Baudelaire what inspiration was, and he responded by saying, "Inspiration is something that commands me to work every single day." And Dostoyevsky said, "Genius is nothing more than a long, sustained patience." What a person has to do is sit himself down before a stack of blank papers, which is in itself terrifying. There is nothing as frightening as a stack of blank pieces of paper and the thought that I have to fill them from top to bottom, placing letters one after the other. . . . and I begin to write. If nothing occurs to me, I remain seated at the writing table until something finally does come to mind.

Flannery O'Connor, short story and novel writer, explained:

Every morning between 9 and 12 I go to my room and sit before a piece of paper. Many times I just sit for three hours with no ideas coming to me. But I know one thing: If an idea does come between 9 and 12, I am there ready for it.

The nineteenth-century prolific British novelist Anthony Trollope said:

A man can always do the work for which his brain is fitted if he will give himself the habit of regarding his work as a normal condition of his life. I therefore venture to advise young men who look forward to authorship as the business of their lives, even when they propose that that authorship be of the highest class known, to avoid enthusiastic rushes with their pens, and to seat themselves at their desks day by day as though they were lawyer's clerks—and so let them sit until the allotted task shall be accomplished.

And in 1996, Amos Oz, Israel's most respected novelist, testified, "I used to feel guilty about an unproductive morning, especially when I lived on the kibbutz, and everyone else was working—ploughing fields, milking cows, planting trees. Now I think of my work as a shopkeeper: it is my job to open up in the morning, sit and wait for customers. If I get some it is a blessed morning, if not, well I'm still doing my job." The British novelist Graham Greene summed it up, "If one wants to write, one simply has to organize one's life in a mass of little habits."

Writers write. It is that simple.

And writers suffer the same problems in getting started as nonwriters. In fact, the more you are published, the higher the expectations placed on you by editors, readers, and yourself and, therefore, the more likely you are to suffer paralysis. We never are prepared enough; never feel we have the authority to be an authority; never believe we write well enough; never have the time, the place, the tools; always have other responsibilities that have to be faced first—and on and on. All the excuses may be legitimate, but writers write despite all the good reasons not to write.

Here are some tricks of the writer's trade that will help get the writing done.

NULLA DIES SINE LINEA

"Never a day without a line" was probably what the ancient cave artists told their young before written history. It was the counsel of Horace, who lived from 65 to 8 B.C., and it is the counsel of writers in every century since. Put rear end in chair every day and keep it there until the writing is done.

Writing becomes relatively easy if writing becomes a daily habit. I write in the morning in my office where I have my computer, my files, my music. I have my own writing ritual: pick out five classical CDs for my carousel player, read and answer e-mail, then attend to the writing task I assigned myself at the end of yesterday's writing. I know the task and my brain has been working on what I may say. Most mornings, the writing flows.

The writing becomes expected in the way you are expected to wait on tables, show up for your job in the emergency room, deliver papers. Roger Simon of the *Baltimore Sun* explained, "There is no such thing as writer's block. My father drove a truck for 40 years. And never once did he wake up in the morning and say: 'I have truck driver's block today. I am not going to work.'"

Most writers, myself included, were late-at-night writers in college. This was true for me also when I first worked on a newspaper. It is a romantic time to write, and I still remember the special feeling of loneliness, of being awake when others sleep, that seemed to encourage great thoughts. But most writers, by the time they are 30, follow the advice of the great German author Goethe who said, "Use the day before the day. Early morning hours have gold in their mouth." John McPhee, the master nonfiction writer, used to loop his bathrobe belt through a chair and tie himself in until the writing was done. Novelist Jessamyn West stayed in her nightclothes until she reached her daily quota. John Hersey, journalist and novelist, said, "To be a writer is to sit down at one's desk in the chill portion of every day, and to write."

ESTABLISH ACHIEVABLE DEADLINES

Most students see deadlines as an enemy. The deadline is my friend. If I do not have a deadline I never finish a piece of writing.

I welcome, in fact insist, that editors give me deadlines. Then I set my own deadline a bit earlier to give myself room for life's interruptions. My Tuesday column for the *Boston Globe* is due by Friday. I deliver it on Monday, nine days ahead of publication. If for some reason—a doctor's appointment, a long weekend, a sick computer—I do not worry. I have plenty of time to write—and rewrite in response to the editor's reading.

I write poems because I have to have a new poem for my poetry group the second and fourth Thursday of the month. I will produce three more books because each has its own deadline.

BREAK A WRITING ASSIGNMENT INTO SMALL DAILY TASKS

Once the deadline is established, I work backward, breaking the project down into a series of small daily tasks. Years ago, a nephew of mine, a psychology professor at the University of New York at Stony Brook, told me that 90 minutes is the maximum learning time for most people. That made me keep track of my writing time for months, and, indeed, 90 minutes was the maximum time I was efficient. In fact, I usually produced drafts in much smaller chunks of time—4 minutes, 7, 12, 20, 30, 45, 60.

I am also most productive when I have a single writing task each day. Sometimes I have to work on two projects—or more—each day, but I do not accomplish as much when this happens. I break long projects into brief daily tasks: "draft lead for Chapter 1," "develop middle of Chapter 1," "get new character on stage in second chapter of novel," "develop hospital scene," "sketch in antipollution argument," "write essay ending." I know the task I am going to be working on the next morning when I leave my writing desk.

I do the same thing with research: "get list of sources from library," "call first three sources," "schedule victim interview," "read brain scan article," "watch operation tape, take notes," "e-mail secondary sources." As a woman rock climber explained as she completed a record several-day climb in California, "You eat an elephant a bite at a time."

KNOW TOMORROW'S TASK TODAY

One of the most important tricks of the writer's trade is, at the end of the writing session, to know the writing task you face when you return to your desk. You don't know what you are going to write—the writing comes in the writing—but you should know the territory and the task. *I'm going to write a Thanksgiving Day column.* I don't know what I'm going to say, but I do know I'm going to deal with the giving of thanks and that it will be done in about 800 words, or the task may be getting a lead and a sketch outline for Chapter 4, developing the middle of Chapter 4, finishing Chapter 4.

REHEARSE

My writing day really begins when I finish the morning's writing. Each morning I discover that the well has filled in the last 24 hours, and I can draw from it because I assigned my conscious, unconscious, and subconscious to play with what I may write tomorrow.

Writing is thinking, and thought does not begin with a conclusion but an itch, a hint, a clue, a question, a doubt, a wonder, a problem, an answer without a question, an image that refuses to be forgotten. I rehearse what I may write, trying out lines, hooking fragments of information together, seeing patterns of meaning in my head, on the 3×5 cards I always carry in my shirt pocket, in my daybook, and, sometimes, on the computer. I silently—and sometimes out loud to my wife's surprise—talk to myself about what I may write.

When I return to my writing desk the next morning I often feel empty, barren of any ideas, but when I start to write I find writing comes to the screen. And if I haven't rehearsed or rehearsal has not worked, I don't wait for an idea; I start writing. Writing produces writing.

A WRITER'S PLACE

A writing room reinforces the writing habit, and I am fortunate these days to have my own writing room under the back porch (with a glass wall that looks out on my woods), my computer, fax, copier, scanner, printer, all my tools as well as my music and my books. But I am not always here and I have learned to create a writing space in an airport or on a plane, in a hotel room or my daughter's dining room table, on a roadside picnic table, or in a doctor's waiting room. If you can't have a room, use a desk in a corner of a room, or a table in the library or cafeteria or an empty classroom you can make into your writing room.

I have a shoulder bag that holds my daybook, calendar/address book, a "to read and edit" file, pens, glue, scissors, and, often, my laptop computer. When I am not traveling the laptop sits beside my chair in the room where we read, watch TV, listen to music. I open up the laptop and have a writing space away from my office. Learn how to make a space where writing will happen.

Each writer has to develop a writing habit, and that pattern will change according to the writer's experience with a writing task, the writer's thinking and working style, as well as the external demands on the writer's time. Develop your own writing habit. Mine keeps changing with experience, new writing tasks, changes in my life, but discipline is essential to the writing and rewriting process. Study the conditions when the writing has gone well and try to reproduce them. And be realistic. Don't try to schedule what will take two hours in fifteen minutes before class or plan your writing time to coincide with the nightly hall hockey game in the dorm.

....

INTERVIEW WITH A PUBLISHED WRITER: ELIZABETH COOKE

I met Elizabeth Cooke when she took a course with me. She was a master teacher of writing and a published writer, and at the end of the course she said she wanted to continue graduate work. I asked what she wanted to do. She said she wanted to write novels. I said, "Go home and write." She did and she has published two novels, *Complicity* and *Zeena*, articles, essays, poetry, and short stories. She teaches writing at the University of Maine at Farmington. "I'm still learning," she tells her students, as she writes alongside them. She has two grown children and she and her husband live in a nineteenth-century farmhouse surrounded by woods, mountains, sky, and a myriad of wildlife, all of which allow her the room to dream and write.

I am one of her students. I mail everything I write to her and learn from her responses. I am delighted she has been willing to be interviewed on rewriting.

How do you find something to write about?

It's not so much a question of "finding" it, as it is listening to it call to me. In fact, I don't think I have ever "tried" to find something to write about. The things I write about come at me—while I am walking in the woods, driving the car, reading my mail, any time at all. Since I don't start with an idea, but with a visual image or a voice, I need to be "listening" all the time. Connected to the image or the voice is a feeling I can't let go of—I may not even know what the feeling is, but something is tugging at me that requires my attention, that says: Put this into words and see what it is.

I began my first novel with an image of two women in a car, driving on a winding New England road in the autumn. I knew the women were mother and daughter; I knew they were heading back to some place they hadn't visited for years. That's all I knew. The feeling of tension between the two women was big as the sky; I was compelled to find out what it was. That's the "finding out" I do.

How do you get over the resistance to write?

In part, I don't. I can always find an excuse—the laundry, my students' essays, a letter to write, a phone call—and often I let those things get in the way of writing. I don't fight it too much because I know that when the thing I am listening for gets loud enough, I won't be able to do those other things anyway. The thing I am listening for will take center stage, and there's nothing I can do then but write. Until I am done with the work, I have no resistance to write. If it's a short story or an essay, it may take a few days or a weeks or months. If it's a novel, it will take a year or more. When the project is done, then I wait for the next calling. Sometimes I wait weeks, sometimes months, but once I get started, the writing comes before all else in my life. Then, I am writing all the time, whether at the computer or not. The writing has taken over.

But how do you get over your resistance to write when you have an assignment as students do?

I try to find my way into the assignment. I try to make it mine. When I was a student, I imagined I was not writing for my professor, but for myself. I asked: What interests me in this question? What do I believe is important here? I got tangled up when I thought about the grade, about whether I was doing the assignment correctly, about whether it was what the professor wanted. If I could let that kind of thinking go (the thinking that censors creativity and exploration) and write because I cared about the subject, I could overcome the resistance to the work.

As a teacher of writing, I tell students, "Follow your interest in the subject. Let the assignment take you somewhere. Let it let you discover what you think."

How do you develop a draft that may be rewritten?

Every draft I write will need to be rewritten—that's what a draft is. It's a start. Then comes the next draft. And the next, and the next. Each draft is *What I Have So Far*. Rewriting is implicit in the word "draft." If writing can be compared to a tree, then revision is its process of leafing out. The first draft might be the wintry tree, branches like lace in the sky, but leafless. Revision fills out the tree, gives the writer the depth and breadth she needs. Revision never stops. Even after something is published, the revising goes on, even if only in the writer's head as she reads the printed words.

The early part of the process is then like this: After I get a possible first line, I write some more, then read what I have written, making changes along the way. Every new word and line requires changes in the lines around it, and maybe even adjusts what I have done in the previous paragraphs. Then I write some more, then read, make changes. Reading over what I have written keeps me on track and helps me go deeper. I have to keep reading the words to tell me what I have said so I can decide if that is what I mean and so I know what to say next.

Once I have a draft, revision begins. I read it so I can know what it is I have, so I can get ready to start again with the first line and go through, line by line, revising, adding new sections, moving lines and sections around, reshaping the development and expanding, always expanding, cutting, always cutting, adjusting, always adjusting as I go along.

How do you know when you need to rewrite?

Ernest Hemingway said it best when he stated that revision is "getting the words right." This is it. So I revise when the words don't sound right in my head; when I read the words and cringe; when I feel gaps open before my eyes; when, as I read the words, I keep wanting to change them, to make them sound better. When I keep thinking, "I'd better show this to so-and-so for another opinion." When I don't know if it's good enough or says what I mean to say.

I don't know what it feels like to *not* need to rewrite, since rewriting is what writing is.

What attitudes do you find helpful as you begin to revise?

In all areas of my life, I am an impatient person. Except in writing, and in the revision that implies. When it comes to writing, I am eternally patient. I forget about time, about responsibilities, about the bread in the oven, about my friend next door who is not feeling well, about my dog who needs a walk. Some might call it selfish, but I call it being patient with the writing.

Some might call it discipline, but I still call it being patient with the writing. Patience is what allows me to linger over a paragraph, to reconsider a line 25 times, to search for a word or the meaning I am trying to find. Patience is returning to the first line over and over again until I am ready to go on. In writing one novel, I spent three months revising the first 12 pages; then I went on to write the rest of the story—over 400 pages—in six months. That's patience.

I love my subjects and want to get the writing as close to "right" as I can. If I don't feel strongly about a subject, if I don't really care, I will let it go. But when I am invested in it, when I believe that what I have to say matters (if only to me), and when I want to find out what it is I am trying to say, then I revise because it's the only way to go.

If I want to see spring come to the wintry tree, I have to draw in the leaves.

What specific process(es) do you try when rewriting?

I rely on line-by-line reading as the basis for all revision. In the single line are the words that tell me what I need to know—Do I need more? Do I need less? Have I gotten it right? What do the words say? Is that exactly what I mean? The word "exactly" is the key—this is the heart of revision for me.

When I change a line, then I go back to the start of the paragraph again and read it through, making more changes. This will often take me back to the previous paragraph, which may take me back to the start of the section or chapter. Over and over, reading, adjusting, reading, adjusting. This is the only revision I know.

Leaving the work for short periods is also helpful to me. This allows the unconscious to get to work, to tell me what I need to know. If I turn my attention to something else—cooking, walking, grading papers, writing a letter—at some point the writing will budge its way into my thoughts. A word, a phrase, a line will come. A piece of information, retrieved from some deep place inside my brain, will nudge me. If I can't go directly to the writing, I jot down the idea. "Leah will write a letter to Will before she leaves home." Or, "Don't forget to include what Lewis said." Or, "More on the motorcycle." If I don't write these thoughts down as they come, I lose them.

Once I have a draft, it is helpful to find a reader I can trust, someone who will act as a mirror to me and tell me what I have done. I don't need a lot of response at this point. I need to know what works, first; what doesn't work, second. Once I learn these things, it's time to go back to the first line of the first page and start in reading and revising against the backdrop of the reader's response.

Revision is, again, a process of being patient so the material can tell me what I need to know.

What tools do you use?

My tools might also be the atmosphere in which I write, the cup of tea I hold against my cheek when I am thinking so the steam rises before my eyes, the books on the shelves beside the place where I write, the photographs on the wall, and the window which opens to a small grassy area, then to woods and sky.

It took me a long time to give up paper and pencil as I composed. The texture of paper, the feel of the pencil in my hand, the beauty of the letters as they were shaped, these were once important tools for me. Now I use paper and pencil only for note taking.

Now the computer, a laptop, is the main concrete tool of writing.

What three things do you wish you'd known as a college student about writing?

Before college I had written poetry, and bits and pieces of essays, on my own; my school experience with writing had been discouraging and disheartening, nearly squashing the wish I had first felt at age 9 to be a writer when it was a fascination with words, a delight in imagination, and a recognition that stories conveyed the human experience that drew me.

Amazingly, in college I learned that academic writing is not the only way to express oneself. In my freshman composition class I wrote personal narrative essays—it was my first school experience with writing about what mattered to me. I learned what it felt like to be immersed in a writing project. I learned the thrill of the private world of writing, that discovery and learning take place for me by writing to find out what I think and know. I learned the importance of shape and form through the discovery of the subject—a revelation! Form follows content, I discovered. There is hope, I thought.

My college writing instructor opened the door to what writing is all about. Though I was given specific assignments, within those assignments was great latitude. I was asked to write a compare/contrast essay, and was given two possible forms for this assignment, but I was allowed to choose my own subject. I was asked to write about a person who had influenced me, but the shape and development of the essay was of my own choosing. I thrived and was successful for the first time in an academic setting.

The rest of my college experience was purely academic; all of it was valuable, but not always for the reasons my instructors intended.

COMMENTARY

Interview yourself about revision to discover what you know that you didn't know. That interview might be about a skill, a job, a hobby you have that would illuminate revision—play rehearsal, sales training, football practice. Interview a writer in town about revision, or a lawyer, engineer, clergyperson, corporate manager who writes. Look up interviews with famous writers in the library, perhaps in the *Paris Review Interviews* to see how what they say relates to what Elizabeth Cooke said. And certainly interview the writers in your class—and invite them to interview you. You may surprise yourself with what you know and say.

CHAPTER 2

REWRITE TO FOCUS

When the ambulance screams up to an accident, the paramedics have to decide which patient is most gravely injured and then they have to decide what is the victim's most serious problem. There are usually cuts and bruises, broken bones, external and internal bleeding, difficulty in breathing. The medics have to decide immediately which problem threatens life and what can be done about it.

When I read first drafts from students, I must sometimes become a writer medic, deciding which section threatens the life of the essay and needs immediate treatment. From my trauma center experience with students and the professional writers I coach, the priority problem is focus.

....

DIAGNOSIS: NO FOCUS

I may see a draft that is sloppily prepared, full of misspellings (and if this poor speller can catch them, the writer is in real trouble), punctuation problems, incorrect facts, illogical structure, and an uneven, awkward style, but underneath it all is a lack of focus. An effective piece of writing says one thing and, before rewriting a draft, you should be able to state it in a single sentence. John Steinbeck used to do just that for each book he wrote, and I have found it helpful in revising an article or a book.

Once you have the focus, everything in the piece should relate to the focus and advance the meaning. Novelist Kurt Vonnegut said, "Don't put anything in a story that does not reveal character or advance the action." It is just as true of nonfiction.

Think of a camera shot. You want the viewer's eye to be led to the significant point: to see how the wedding photo reveals how close—or how far apart—they stand; to capture the look on the bride's mother's face; to capture the best man's desperate search for the ring; to see the bride's bouquet arcing through the air and the faces watching it.

The focus is the meaning of the story, essay, term paper, memo, poem. The focus captures the reader's attention and holds it through the piece of writing. It answers the reader's question, "Why should I be reading this?"

THE ELEMENTS OF AN EFFECTIVE FOCUS

An effective focus should be clear. You shouldn't have to think a long time after reading a draft to find a possible focus. Be able to say in just one sentence what the draft means. Readers will not make that effort; they will just stop reading.

To discover and state the focus, be able to answer the following questions with a specific, brief statement: a sentence or less.

What Is the Single, Dominant Meaning?

Every piece of effective writing will say many different things to individual readers. Good writing has depth and texture, but something should stand out.

The account of a beach party may include interesting material on who was there; how they dressed; how they behaved; what, and how much, was eaten or drunk; what the swimming was like; what games were played; who came with whom; and who went home with whom; but the account must have a meaning, and the meaning might be hidden in the abundance of all the details of the party. And these details may appear joyful, until the person looking back finds he is writing of a date rape.

What Is the Central Tension Within the Dominant Meaning?

The central tension is what makes the focus dynamic, active, something worth writing—and reading. There should be forces at work within the focus: a question, a doubt, a conflict, a contradiction. The focus should not be a label, *Mom,* but contain a tension: *Mother's First Love: Her Fourth Husband.*

The problem of date rape, for example, is a serious one, but that label will not attract, hold, and influence readers. Effective writing contains a central tension that puts everything in the article in a different perspective. That central tension might be "Beer doesn't make no, yes." The alcoholic hilarity of the outing suddenly turns false and dark—ominous, not celebratory.

The argument might focus on the reader who thinks women say "no" and mean "yes" and therefore a few beers "to loosen her up" justifies a sexual attack: she really wanted it. The account might show how dress and behavior do not justify sexual assault. There is tension in the topic because we discover that the attacker sees a pattern of seduction that the victim does not intend.

What Do Test Readers Say Is the Meaning of the Draft?

It is often helpful to get someone who is not familiar or sympathetic to read a draft and then tell the writer, in a sentence, what it means. I am careful about the person I choose to be a test reader. The person does not need to be an authority on the subject and, in fact, it is often better if the person is not, as my readers will not be. My test readers are not always writers, but they are people who can listen to what I want of them, and respond helpfully to an early draft. If I ask simply if they get the meaning, then they do not immediately jump in and correct my typing and my spelling. They give a candid response to the question I ask. Most of all, the test readers I return to are those who make me want to write as soon as I leave them. They may praise or criticize, but they inspire me to go to work revising the draft.

When a test reader gives me a meaning I did not intend—"Rape is OK at a beach party"—my first tendency is to say, "bad reader," but that is not good enough. The writer has to communicate to readers who are rushed and harried, not interested in the subject, or opposed to the writer's views. It is the responsibility of the writer to create a focus that will be clear to many readers, good or bad, interested or disinterested. Sometimes there are poor or eccentric readings of a draft, but most times when a test reader gives a meaning you do not expect, you can scan the piece and discover the focus is not what you meant. Then you can point the draft in the direction you want.

IF THE DIAGNOSIS IS POSITIVE

If the draft has a clear focus, then move on to the next step in the revision process. Each draft will have its own problems as it passes through revision. The effective writer moves over those stages in the process where a quick diagnosis reveals no problem.

··

SAY ONE THING

One of the biggest differences between the successful writer and the unsuccessful one is that the successful writer says one thing. One idea dominates.

The writer may have known that single idea before writing. It may have come clear to the writer during the writing. Or the idea may be discovered through the reading of the draft. But once the idea is recognized, it has to be developed and clarified by revision.

HOW CAN I FIND THAT ONE THING?

It is vital to articulate the one thing that brings all the issues in the subject into focus. Some of the techniques I use to do this follow.

Questions to Reveal the Focus

Sometimes it is a good idea to back off, turn the draft over, or store it so it is not on the screen. Then think about the subject. After writing and reading the piece, ask yourself:

- What surprised you?
- What did you expect to read? How was what you read different from your expectations?
- What do you remember most vividly?
- What did you learn from the writing and the reading?
- What one thing does a reader need to know?
- What is the single most important detail, quote, fact, idea in the draft?
- What do you itch to explore through revision?
- What single message may the final draft deliver?

Sharpen the Focus

Once you have an answer to those questions, then you can sharpen the focus. Here are some rules for sharpening the focus:

- Use as few words as possible.
- Play with specifics from both sides of the issue that are in tension; avoid generalizations and abstractions.
- Use nouns and verbs, especially active verbs.
- Reveal the central tension.

For example, a student might write: "I'm against violence of any kind. In my experience, and in the opinion of clergy of all faiths as well as sociological studies, it doesn't work. Forget if human beings get maimed or dead and all those human concerns. Figure some people got to get hurt. But I know, from personal experience, that hurting someone physically hurts them mentally but does not make them behave. And it may make the victim as well violent, continuing the circle." *After a conference with a teacher or classmate who said,* "I'm confused. What are you trying to say—what is the writing telling you to write?" *the student might try a more focused approach:* "The more my father beat me to keep me off the streets, the more I fled to the streets. We live in a violent society and the arguments against violence are all idealistic. My argument against violence is pragmatic, no idealism involved: violence doesn't work."

Titles and First Lines

The focused meaning may, in fact, become the title. When I was freelancing magazine articles, I would start writing an article by brainstorming 100 to 150 possible titles, in fragments of time as the research was winding down. Each title was a window into the draft I might write.

To brainstorm, you have to be willing to be silly, knowing that in this freedom may lie an important insight. If I was assigned to write a paper on roommates, I might start with titles that would remind me of experiences—and problems and conflicts and satisfactions—I had with roommates.

My Roommate for 43 Years

My 40 Army Roommates

Why We Had a Fistfight

My Roommates Smell

Snores

Snores and Bores

Don't Room with a Philosopher

Familiarity Breeds Familiarity

Ten Rules for My Roommate

How to Drive a Roommate Crazy

Talk's OK—But at 3 AM?

My Roommate's Snake

My Roommate's Brother

Why I Murdered My Roommate

Why I Murdered My Roommate—and Was Acquitted

Roommate or Cellmate?

Cheese, Toothpaste, and Computers

The Music Wars

Jazz Rock Folk Classical

Rocking to Mozart

One Roommate and Four Alarm Clocks

When His Lover Stays Overnight
The Importance of Privacy
No Passion Please
Living in My Roommate's Plant Jungle
The Poster Wars
Borrow My Boyfriend, Not My Jeans
What's Hers Is Hers; What's Mine Is Hers

You could go on and on, and so could I. I may, for example, write a humorous column about my wife, my roommate for 43 years, in the form of advice to freshmen meeting their roommates for the first time. I could write a nostalgic essay, with some bite, about the roommate with whom I had a fight. I might even write about my experiences in an army barracks with 40 roommates or in a foxhole in combat with one. I am not restricted to my list. I might find myself writing about some of the office mates I've suffered and how they suffered me.

Join me in the game of titles. I used to do 150 or so at a run. And what if number 3 of 150 is the best? Well, now you know it! The discarded titles may turn up as lines in the article or as starting places for other articles.

The fragments of language that focus meaning often become the first lines of a piece of writing. As a journalist, I am a great believer in writing the lead—the first line, the first paragraph or three, the first page—first. Let's see what happens if I write a few leads for that roommate column:

> As our grandchildren go off to college for the first time, those of us who have the same roommate for 40, 50 years, or more should share our cohabitation wisdom.

***

> Selective vision—or elective blindness—is the first quality a student should develop in facing a college roommate for the first time.

I do not see the ironing we brought from New Jersey in 1963 that adorns one corner of our bedroom, and Minnie Mae, of course, will eventually learn not to mention my . . .

***

My first college roommate and I got along after we had a genuine, male, prancing-around, dirty-words fistfight in our closet of a room.

Now, seeing freshmen arrive in cars hung with furniture, I realize their adjustment won't be to calculus, rhetoric, the philosophy of Hegel, but to fitting into a small room with a stranger who will get larger, louder, more difficult every day.

***

I've heard of people who keep in touch with their college roommates decade by decade and I've heard of hostage victims who grow fond of their captors, but one of the good things about getting old is that I will never ever have to have a roommate again. I hope.

Perhaps in the nursing home, but I won't talk about that yet. And I am happy to have a mate, but it is fortunate we live in nine rooms, not one.

***

The first great lesson of college is that someone with a sense of humor—or sadistic need to cause trouble—has locked you and your roommate into a small space for a long year.

Now I have had a roommate for 41 years, and we are still working out all those trivial issues of territory that are so important to the human animal. As a full-grown, white-bearded sage, I have some wise counsel for first-year college students who face the first test of university life: I am supposed to live with. . .

***

The first great lesson of college is that someone with a sense of humor or sadistic need to cause trouble has locked you and your roommate into a small space for a long year.

~~Now~~ I have had a roommate for 45 years, and ~~we are still working out all those trivial issues of territory that are so important to the human animal. As a full-grown, white-bearded sage,~~ I have ~~some wise counsel~~ advice for first-year college students who face their first ~~test of university life — I am supposed to live with . . .~~ roommate.

What have I been doing? Playing my way into an essay, trying on beginning points, voices, ideas the way you try on clothes before a party. Each lead gives me a direction in which I might go. The entire piece of writing grows out of the beginning that establishes the following:

- the question in the reader's mind to be answered in the draft
- the authority of the writer to answer it
- the direction of the draft
- the pace of the writing
- the form
- the voice

BUT WHAT ABOUT ALL THE OTHER GOOD STUFF?

There are two kinds of good stuff. One kind can be used to support and advance the focus of the story, to clarify and communicate your meaning. The other is material that will draw the reader's mind away from your message.

Supporting Material

Every piece of information, every literary device, every line, and every word must support, develop, and communicate the meaning. Each comma, verb, statistic, reference, descriptive detail, transition, summary sentence should relate in a direct way to the central tension of what is being written.

The melody by itself is hardly enough. The meaning, focused and sharpened, needs all the supporting material to reveal its full significance and to make the reader react emotionally and intellectually.

Distracting Material

The material you have collected through research and the thinking you have done through writing that must be cut from the draft, however, is not wasted. It is all money in the bank. You may not spend it on this draft, but it is there, to be drawn on in the future.

And in a way it is still in the draft, even after it has been cut. The marble that has been cut away from the statue made an essential contribution to the statue. It is there in the revealing.

....

FRAME YOUR MEANING

You may not know much about writing, but I bet you know how to frame a picture with a camera. If you want to reveal the tranquil beauty of a flowery meadow, make sure you have not included the blur of traffic on the highway beside the meadow. If you want to comment on modern life by showing the cars rushing by unseeing, make sure you get both highway and meadow and you use an exposure that will show the cars blurring past the stationary beauty of the wildflowers in the meadow. That is what the writer does. For example, you might start an essay—or a short story—in either of these frames:

> It was not the commute between home and office and hospital that made it possible for him to survive, but the ritual he followed every day when he pulled off the highway and studied the tranquil beauty of a meadow that had escaped the march of the malls. Some people liked water, but he drew strength from the ocean swell of land, the dance of wind on tall grass, the yearly explosion of wildflowers, each in its season.

***

> First the highway amputating this meadow from his grandfather's farm, then the subdivision behind the meadow, the strip mall on the left, the fast-food place on the right, the hundreds upon hundreds of people who raced by this last meadow, not seeing the way it changed its color, hour by hour, under wind

and sky, ignoring its tranquil beauty undisturbed until the annual explosion of wildflowers, promiscuous, profligate, so much more necessary to humans than highways and burgers and cheap clothes and houses decorated with plastic possessions.

It helps us to realize how much we know about writing, without knowing we know it, when we use one art or craft and adapt its lessons, in this case focus, to our writing. Writing and rewriting go better when we can face our tasks with confidence. And we may not feel confident about our writing, but many of us feel confident with a camera in hand.

WHAT TO LEAVE OUT

Draw a frame around the subject. You can even do this physically, by scanning the draft and drawing a line through everything that has to go. Sometimes I circle the material and mark it with an arrow heading off the page, or a question mark. Most times the decision is easy, but sometimes I have to scan the draft a number of times to see if it should go or remain.

WHAT TO KEEP IN

Keep in what moves your meaning forward. The remaining material must develop and communicate the focused meaning.

"But almost everything went. My draft has shrunk!"

Good. This is an important stage in the writing process. When we have found our focus, it gives us space for complete development. Maybe half the material can be saved, or only a third, or a quarter—a page? Now you have room for the material you will add during the revision process.

Revision for the experienced writer is often a far more radical process than the inexperienced writer imagines. The experienced writer knows that to cut often means to reveal. Once I cut 237 pages from a draft in response to a modest but perceptive comment by a horrified editor. It *did* improve the book. The master writer knows that what is taken out is necessary to get the draft to the place where it can be made to work. The writing that is cut isn't a sign of failure but progress toward an effective final draft.

Most of us write a first draft that skims over the surface of our topic. That's appropriate. We are searching for our focus, our meaning. Once we find it, then a lot of the material we included can be jettisoned. Over the side with it. No regrets.

....

SET THE DISTANCE

An important issue relating to focus that is rarely discussed in most textbooks is the matter of distance. We can stand nose to nose with our subject or back off and see it from a mountaintop, a space shuttle, or even, by writing from a historical perspective, from a distance of hundreds of years.

The focus, as in a camera, depends on how far away you—and the reader—stand from the subject. The distance cannot be set by a rule book but depends on the subject, your purpose in writing about the subject, and the reader.

WHEN TO USE CLOSE-UPS

Close-ups bring immediacy. We do not photograph the field of spring flowers but move in on one poppy, show the whole blossom or go even closer to a petal, perhaps catching a bee stopping by for breakfast. In the close-up we don't look at the entire government but the legislature, not the House of Representatives and the Senate but the Senate only, not the committee structure but a committee, not the committee but a single senator, not the career of the senator but one revealing vote.

We can, with the close-up, expose the details of a scene, a law, a scientific experiment, a crime, a vote. We can reveal complexity and simplicity, cause and effect, action and reaction.

WHEN TO STEP BACK

We step back when we take a snapshot of a single wildflower and then show the fields of wildflowers that stretch for miles to the Rockies. We show the historical and theological roots of the abortion issue and the pressures that caused the senator to take a position and now reverse it. The distance shot allows us to make the generalization from the documentation: to put the anecdote, the quotation, the statistic, the scientific discovery in perspective. We can show what came before and predict what will follow. We provide a context. But what if I need to do both?

WHEN TO ZOOM

You have a zoom lens. Use it. Don't just stand in one spot and try to see what's going on from there. Take your reader in close for emphasis, for clarity, for dramatic effect, to make the reader think and feel. Then zoom back so the reader understands the full implications of what the reader has been shown. In every war, photographers and writers use zoom techniques to reveal the landscape of war; then they move in close to see the wounded or the dead, which reveals the price of war in individual human terms; then they zoom out again to show the larger context of war.

Don't move in and back wildly, without purpose, like Uncle Max with his new video camera at the wedding. Move smoothly in close. Draw back halfway—in close once more—then back again in a pattern that serves the reader, giving the reader the information and the experience the reader needs to become involved in your subject.

Make believe you are a movie director, as I often do when I am writing, and make a sketch showing the camera angle: what it includes and excludes. Then move the camera to different positions to see what is emphasized, included, excluded.

THE IMPORTANCE OF FOCUS

Drafting is putting in, but revision is the craft of selection. Revising a draft takes hundreds of executive selections. Each word may affect the meaning of the word next to it and words a page away; each line has implications for other lines; each sentence and paragraph changes the emphasis, pace, impact of other sentences and paragraphs; each piece of information influences the value of other pieces of information. How do you make these decisions? Use focus. Every decision is resolved by its value to developing and communicating your focused meaning.

REVISING ACADEMIC WRITING

Academic writing is intellectual writing, a mind speaking to a mind. In nonacademic writing we usually appeal to the mind and the heart, trying to stimulate the reader's emotions and thoughts. In writing within the academic community, the appeal is to thought. And focus is of primary importance.

Much academic writing is argumentative in the sense that the writing attacks a previous opinion or establishes an opinion that withstands attack. In each case there must be a clear focus—a thesis—that is stated, defined, developed, and supported with objective evidence. Remember Vonnegut: everything must relate to the thesis.

In the graceful essay, the lyric poem, the dramatic scene, the focus is often not stated. It is implied. The reader is given an artistic experience that stimulates the focus. The pages illuminate the reader's own experience. In academic writing, however, the thesis is clearly stated, and often restated during the development of the research paper, the blue book exam, the term paper, the final master's degree paper that is called a thesis. It might be called a focus.

The academic reader expects the writer to not only have a focus, but a train of logic that carries the reader toward agreement with thesis, or focus.

INTERVIEW WITH A PUBLISHED WRITER: CHRISTOPHER SCANLAN

I first met Chip Scanlan when I was appointed writing coach for the *Providence Journal.* He was the reporter most interested in the writing process—and the most critical. In Providence he helped create and run the paper's writing program and edited *How I Wrote the Story,* a collection of newswriting accounts. Our professional dialogue remains at the center of our relationship that has grown so that if I had to choose, he would be my closest friend. We talked about our craft almost daily as he moved from the *Providence Journal* in Rhode Island to the *St. Petersburg Times* in Florida, then to the District of Columbia where he was a national correspondent in the Washington bureau of Knight-Ridder newspapers. He created the bureau's first family beat and won awards for coverage of veterans' health care and consumer issues and a Robert F. Kennedy award for international journalism for a series on hazardous exports. Scanlan is now director of writing programs at The Poynter Institute in St. Petersburg, Florida, a nonprofit educational institution that provides seminars for recent college graduates and newspaper professionals. He is also editor of the annual *Best Newspaper Writing.* His articles, essays, and short stories have appeared in the *Washington Post Magazine,* the *Boston Globe Magazine, Redbook,* and *Delaware Today.* He is writing a journalism textbook for Harcourt Brace College Publishers.

What techniques do you use to find a focus before writing a first draft?

I tend to over-report every story, as a glance at my desk demonstrates. Archeologists could find evidence of earlier civilizations in the layers of notebooks, reports, books, newspapers, magazines, Post-it Notes, binders, file folders that accumulate when I am reporting a story. Reporting helps me understand a subject, but after a while it begins to overwhelm me and confusion sets in. What does all this mean? What was my story anyway? What's the significance of the interview notes, statistics, observations, and descriptions I've spent so much time collecting?

The only way out of it is to push all of it aside and go to the one source that knows it all—me—and start asking the questions that help me discover the heart of the story, the single, dominant impression that every effective story conveys. *What's the news? What's the story?*

What image captures the story for me? What quote, or better, what dialogue between more than one person, sums it all up? I try to keep in mind what Thomas Boswell, a terrific sports columnist for the *Washington Post,* once said: "The most important thing in the story is finding the central idea. It's one thing to be given a topic, but you have to find the idea or the concept within that topic. Once you find that idea or thread, all the other anecdotes, illustrations, and quotes are pearls that hang on this thread. The thread may seem very humble, the pearls may seem very flashy, but it's still the thread that makes the necklace."

Here are some techniques that work for me:

- Write your story in six words.
- Write a budget line, the sentence that promises a specific approach before the story is written.
- Ask two questions that keep track of the focus of any story: *What's the news? What's the story?* They address the reader's concerns: What's new here? What's this story about? Why am I reading this?

How do you know you need to revise for focus after you have finished a draft?

I generally have two reactions to story drafts: pride or disgust. I've learned, through long and sometimes bitter experience, to be suspicious when I think the draft is good because it won't be long before I see its true flaws. When I'm disgusted with the writing, I know I'm on the right track. If I can't stand to read it aloud, have an overwhelming urge to tear it up or hit the delete key until the computer screen is blank, then I know my focus is off. Whatever I want to say or need to say in the story is not being said, and I need to sit back and ask myself a simple question, "What is it you're trying to say?" Invariably, the sentence I write in response articulates in a phrase the central meaning of the story. It's often something I've been trying to avoid saying for some reason.

What attitudes do you find helpful as you try to focus a draft?

I was fortunate to work for eight years with one of the best newspaper editors in America, Joel Rawson, executive editor of the *Providence Journal.* I can still remember the intensity of the question that he was always asking at every stage of the process, from reporting to rewriting: "What's this story about?" Or to be more precise, he'd lean toward me and demand, "Do you know what this story is about?" Then he'd proceed to teach me the universal theme that lurked beneath the topic. Joel taught me to dig deep, to look for the universal in the specific, to make the human connection, to never stop until I knew the basic theme of my story. The attitudes needed are persistence and empathy. The focus of a story usually resides in the pit of my stomach. When I feel it there, almost like an electrical current, then I know I have the focus.

What specific process—or processes—do you try to focus a draft?

I usually begin by freewriting; that is, I try to discover the focus by writing and seeing what comes out. I am looking for words, ideas, combinations that surprise me. If I'm bored by my writing, why should anyone else care? If I can surprise myself, then I have a better chance to surprise my reader.

What tools do you use when searching for a focus?

- Questions and more questions. What's the news? What's the story? What am I trying to say? How do I want people to respond when they're finished reading the story? What's the best headline or title? Who's this story about? Why am I writing this story?
- Freewriting. Essentially I babble on my computer screen.
- Write a headline or a title.
- Talk about my story with an editor, my wife, or a good friend.

How do you know when you have solved the problem of focus?

Carol Knopes, news cover story editor for *USA Today,* says, "the job of a writer is to put elephants into ring boxes." The elephant—that immense load of reporting you've done—must somehow fit into that ring box, a space of perhaps 400 to 800 words. The focus of a story helps you decide what to leave out. If it doesn't relate to the single dominant message, then it doesn't make it.

What are the most important three things you've learned as a publishing writer you wish you knew as a college freshman?

1. Writing is hard work, but it's fun. Keep at it. Don't give up hope. Lower your standards, as poet William Stafford advised. Give yourself a break: what you write today is what you're capable of writing. Strive to improve, but accept what you produce.
2. Good writing may be magical, but it's not magic. It's a rational series of decisions and actions that can be observed, learned, and repeated.
3. All writing is rewriting.

COMMENTARY

I keep learning about focus from professionals such as Chip Scanlan, who teaches journalists to find the focus under the immediate pressures of news deadlines—*What's the news? What's the story?*—that applies to the research paper, the memo, the argument, the critical essay. And I extend my search for how to find a focus by looking at photographs, reading interviews with photographers, studying drawings and paintings, reading what artists have to say, and listening to performers and athletes as they describe the process they go through to achieve focus.

CHAPTER 3

REWRITE TO COLLECT

Writers don't write with words.

Writers write with information: accurate, specific, significant information. It is essential to the craft of revision to consider the information communicated in the draft. Words are the symbols for information, and when there is no information behind the words, the draft is like a check with no money in the account: worthless.

Effective writing serves the reader information the reader can use to understand the world, to think more clearly, to make better decisions, to learn, to act, to appreciate and enjoy life, to become an authority in the eyes of those around the reader. The list of reasons why readers want and need information is long. Effective writing is constructed from sturdy bits of information. Beginning writers can easily understand the necessity for specific information in nonfiction articles designed to communicate information—the research paper, laboratory report, minutes of a meeting—but they have less understanding of the need for information when writing about ideas or feelings. Yet specific information is absolutely essential in both forms of writing.

Which of the following examples from a history of World War II would you read?

> Tech-strategists retroactively engaged in cognitive studies of an interdisciplinary nature theorized that the late entry of U.S. forces, the very lack of preparedness that was so castigated was,

in contradiction to all expectation, a situation that produced positive, if unexpected, tactical and strategic results.

or

Hitler was prepared for war, and when his Stukas and Messerschmitts overran the low countries of northern Europe, the U.S. Air Corps could not have flown with them even if the United States was in the war. Ironically, those who mobilize last will enter combat with the "latest" equipment. If the enemy can be held at bay, the later entry will fly planes, as we did, that are technologically better than the German planes that seemed invincible a year or two earlier. Some scholars have argued that poor preparation is the best preparation for war.

I try to write of my feelings about being unable to help my 20-year-old daughter when she became ill and died. Which example is more effective?

A parent always wants to protect a child and never, no matter how irrational it is, stops feeling guilty if a child is killed or dies from an illness, feeling there must have been something the parent could have done.

or

Lee

Remember me not
when I was kept from you
in the waiting room, not
when I sat in an office signing
your dying, not
when I pushed you on the swing
higher than you had ever flown
and you looked back as I grew small,
certain I would always be able
to save you.

Effective writers of nonfiction, fiction, and poetry do not tell the reader how to feel but give the reader the specific information to make the reader feel.

DIAGNOSIS: TOO LITTLE INFORMATION

Quickly read through your draft and put a check in the left-hand margin whenever you give the reader specific, accurate information. Then go through it again and put a small arrow where you could give the reader specific information that would help the reader, think, feel, experience the draft.

Some of the forms of information the reader may need are revealing detail, fact, statistic, direct quotation, anecdote, firsthand observation, precise definition, attribution, and authoritative citation or reference. Information may take many forms, of course, and may be incorporated into the draft. A book about the writing process might be written on the basis of research reports and have many footnotes and other forms of attribution; this textbook is written from personal experience and has few references to other sources. Neither way is right or wrong; each is appropriate to the forms of writing.

There is no quota on the amount of information needed in a given piece of writing, but if you have pages or paragraphs without checks, then you should read the draft to see if the reader needs more specific information.

THE IMPORTANCE OF INFORMATION

It is normal for inexperienced writers—and some not so inexperienced—to become infatuated with words. The condition is called "word drunk." The writer staggers down the page, spouting words that may, accidentally, sound wonderful but say nothing. Most readers do not want a word-drunk writer any more than they want a shaky-handed surgeon. Here are some of the reasons that it is essential to write with information.

PROVIDES READER SATISFACTION

Readers are hungry for information. They want the images and facts, revealing details and interesting quotations, amazing statistics and insights that make them see, feel, and know their world better than they did before the reading.

It helps to understand the reader's desire for information when you realize that one reason you read is to become an authority. The information-rich writer makes the reader an authority, and the reader, in turn, becomes an authority. The reader broadcasts new information to family, colleagues, friends, and gains status in the process. Joe is in the know; Belinda is in the loop. A good piece of writing ignites a chain reaction of communication. Most of the writing that satisfies us as readers has served us an abundance of information.

ESTABLISHES AUTHORITY

Readers believe specific information. If you want to lie, lie with statistics. Precise information makes the reader believe that you know your stuff. But serve up one piece of precise information that the reader knows is wrong, and the reader won't believe anything in your draft.

Accurate information is the reason that readers trust the writer; inaccurate information is the reason that readers mistrust the writer. Readers test the draft by noting the information that relates to their world. When I read something about a newspaper or a university— both are places I've worked before—I am especially critical. If I think the writer is on target, I trust the writer's comments about institutions I do not know well; but if the writer's comments do not fit my knowledge of newspapers or universities, then I suspect everything the writer says.

PRODUCES LIVELY WRITING

"How can I make my writing lively? It is dull, dull, dull."

Yesterday I was asked that question and I answered, "By concrete details more than anything else. Lively writing is specific, not vague, abstract, and general. It builds the generalizations on the page and in the reader's mind from specific pieces of information that surprise and delight the reader." Often I remind myself of the importance of specifics by taking a piece of writing I particularly like and circling the specific pieces of information.

....

THE QUALITIES OF EFFECTIVE INFORMATION

Effective information is information the reader uses successfully. A manual tells the reader how to solve a problem with computer software; an editorial makes the reader change a vote; a biography puts a historical figure in perspective; a literature textbook illuminates a poem; the poem makes the reader see the woods the reader passes every day with increased perception.

ACCURACY

Readers respect specific information because the author takes the risk of being specific. Much of what pours through our ears is purposely vague, general, abstract; the writer uses politic language that can't be nailed down, information for which the writer is not accountable. Specific writing is unusual, and readers like it, but it must be correct. One slip, as we have said, and the reader will not trust anything the writer says.

Factual Accuracy

The first accuracy is the truth of the fact: the number of miles in the marathon, the cost of the school bond issue, the day of the Battle of Gettysburg, the ingredients in the formula and their precise amounts, what the president actually said in the speech. All must be right. These facts can be checked with authoritative sources and should be. Often the writer will check the source with another source; just because a fact is in print doesn't mean it is a fact.

Here are some questions that you can ask of a fact, then check and recheck if the answer is not "yes":

- Does it make any sense?
- Does it seem possible from what you know of the subject?
- Is it consistent with other facts you know are correct; does it fit the pattern?

- If this fact is true, does it change other facts in the draft—or the meaning of the draft?

Of course, the most interesting and significant facts will not get a simple "yes," but those pieces of information will have to face the skepticism of the reader. They deserve to be checked and rechecked.

Contextual Accuracy

The writer has the responsibility to make sure the information in the text is *accurate in context.* Your campus may have had 73 sexual attacks reported last semester. That statistic may be accurate in fact, but the context may change the impact of that figure. A historical context may reveal that there were 214 attacks two semesters ago and that an educational program seems to be working. Or the 73 attacks reported may be up from 36 but reveal that women are now willing, because of a new reporting procedure that protects their identity, to report sexual attacks.

The context reveals the significance of information. That is a far more difficult, and more important, task than just checking the number of pork pies at a church supper. Here are some questions that may help you test the contextual accuracy of a specific piece of information:

- What does this detail mean to the reader? What message does it deliver to the reader?
- What does this specific detail make the reader think? Feel?
- What impression is conveyed by this specific detail and the information that surrounds it?
- What is the pattern of meaning being built by this piece of information and the specifics that come before and after it?
- Is this piece of information accurate in context?

You are using specific information to construct a meaning, and you have the obligation to make that meaning true.

SPECIFICITY

We like specific information because it catches our eye, or ear; sets off chain reactions of memory or imagination; gives us something to play with; makes us think and feel.

The Disadvantages of General Information

Writers—and politicians, corporate executives, educational administrators, bureaucrats—often use generalizations to avoid responsibility. You can't nail a generalization down. Watch a political press conference. Either party will do.

Meanings, feelings, ideas, generalizations, theories, abstractions are all important. We use them in writing, but we are fortunate when we can cause them to happen in the reader's mind because of what we have said on the page. The details are arranged in a pattern, and that pattern makes the reader construct a meaning or experience a feeling. We cannot usually construct a meaning from generalities. Nothing is there to cause a thought. There is just someone else's thought to be accepted or rejected. It is given to us without documentation. We can't see backstage to discover—and evaluate—how it was put together.

Undocumented generalizations, those not built out of accurate, checkable, specific information in front of your eyes, are weak, flabby, vague, dull. And the writing is as well.

The Advantages of Revealing Details

A revealing detail is a specific that says more than one would expect. "The additive may cause genetic problems" sounds specific, but notice the difference when you read "Urgatative, a normal food additive, may cause nerve damage in a pregnant woman and her child—and her child's child." Revealing details expose the subject; they connect with other details to construct an opinion, argument, theory, poem, story, report that can be studied, challenged, tested.

The details themselves have power. *"The mayor won"* is not equal to *"The mayor won five votes to her opponent's one."* And details can make the reader think beyond the end of the sentence: *"The first African American to be elected mayor won with 71 percent of the white vote.*" Or make the reader feel: *"In her victory statement she thanked her husband, her children, her parents, her campaign workers, and then I lifted Soozie, her Seeing Eye dog, up on her hind legs so she could acknowledge the cheers of the mayor's supporters."*

SIGNIFICANCE

Effective information is significant. If the new mayor had a dog named Soozie, that would mean nothing, but the fact she is a Seeing Eye dog makes a statement about the possibilities for the disabled—a term the mayor never uses—and implies that her administration will pay attention to that minority as well.

Resonance

A powerful detail has resonance; it radiates with implication. Resonance means that when the reader absorbs the information, it increases in importance. We read "She became pregnant at 12 years of age—two years earlier than when her mother had her"—and realize there is a family history. The baby is going to have a baby and a 26-year-old woman is about to become a grandmother. These facts give off an explosion of implication in the reader's mind. Resonance causes the reader to begin thinking, taking the text of the page and exploring its implications.

The newly elected mayor reminds the audience that she went to school in this city, but that although each year the white high school students elected a mayor who served for a day in City Hall, she was not allowed to serve when her African American classmates elected her their mayor. That piece of information resonates. The reader can imagine how she felt then and how she feels now; can imagine the struggle that put her where she is now; can imagine how many other talented citizens did not and do not have the chance to serve; can imagine the changes that allowed this to happen and the changes that need to take place.

Connection

The information you choose should make significant connections in the writer's mind and in the reader's.

With Topic. The information should relate to the topic and advance its meaning in the reader's mind. Often writers collect interesting information and they can't let go of it. The more interesting it is, the more it draws the reader's mind away from the message you are delivering. Each specific should amplify, clarify, extend the topic.

With Other Information. The specific details should work with the other pieces of information in the draft. They should build toward an increasing understanding of the meaning that your draft is delivering to the reader. Some details will increase the impact of the other details; other specifics will qualify or limit the meaning that is building up. During revision you have the opportunity to check on these relationships.

With Reader. The information you choose to use should relate to the reader. Both the type of information—statistics, anecdotes, quotations—and the meaning the information bears should appeal to the reader. What will persuade one reader may turn another off. It is your job to select appropriate information from which to construct your draft.

FAIRNESS

The best way to evaluate the fairness of a draft is to stand back and become a person in the piece of writing or someone who is affected by it. What would you think if you were in the piece or if your reputation were affected by its publication?

THE BASIC FORMS OF INFORMATION

We deal with information all the time, but we don't think of it as information we might use to construct a piece of writing. It may be a good idea to remind ourselves of the common forms of information.

Fact: A precise piece of information that can be documented by independent sources. Linda J. Stone was *elected governor.*

Statistic: A numerical fact. The governor received *5,476,221* votes.

Quotation: The direct statement by an individual speaker or writer or from a document, book, article, report. *"The first Monday of every month the door to my office will be open to any citizen who wishes to see me."*

Anecdote: A brief story or narrative which makes a point that documents the point a writer is making. The parables, such as the story of the loaves and fishes in the Bible, are a form of the anecdote. *"Governor-elect Stone drove the family car, a five-year-old Ford station wagon with 137,422 miles on it, to election headquarters herself."*

Descriptive detail: A specific that reveals a person, place, or event. She held high the *"old-fashioned wooden clipboard"* she carried during the campaign on which she had made notes on what individual citizens told her during the morning coffee meetings she held in private homes, offices, schools, and factories.

Authoritative report: A document that is accepted as accurate by a responsible organization such as a court, corporation, or academic discipline. In her acceptance speech, Governor-elect Stone cited the *"Newkirk Report that called for small classes in the public school system and a paid-by-the-state system of summer retraining for teachers."*

Common information: Information the reader can be assumed to know: three strikes and you're out; the president outranks the vice president. *"The governor-elect of this state is immediately given a state police driver and an official limousine."*

These are just a few of the most common forms of information. There are obviously many more, and I have used a journalistic example common to all of us. Each academic discipline, each corporation, each profession, each government agency will have its own basic inventory of information forms. Most of them will, however, fit these patterns. The literary scholar will have many quotations from the work studied and from its critics; the economist will cite many statistics; the physicist will have many facts, mostly in the language of mathematics; the environmentalist will build a draft with many descriptive details; the historian will make good use of authoritative reports; the case worker may have a great deal of anecdotal evidence. In every case, however, the most effective pieces of writing will be constructed with specific information.

WHERE DO YOU FIND INFORMATION?

One of the reasons I am glad to be a writer is that I am forced to continue to learn. I have to search my world for the specifics I can use to discover what I have to say. The process of writing is a process of thinking, but if the thinking is to be effective—and if readers are going to read and use it—it must be built from information. And to get that information I have to study my subject.

MEMORY

We fear that writing will prove us ignorant. But writers discover how much we know by writing. I don't think I remember what it was like when my father, during the Depression, was fired again and again. Then I write about one of the times and begin to hear him blaming others, never himself, bragging how he told his boss off, how the reason he was fired was that he would be replaced by a "college man." I find out that I remember more than I thought I would, and I also realize I can now begin to recreate my doubts and questions about my father, how I felt, how I would try to live my life. Writing reveals how much I know. Of course, writing may reveal my childhood, but it will never reveal nuclear physics, no matter how many drafts I create. Drafts reveal the knowledge of which you were unaware, not the knowledge you do not possess. If your draft did not show you how much you knew, you may need to take a step back and discover what you know that you didn't know you knew.

Before Writing

I start withdrawing information from my memory bank by brainstorming a list, putting down everything I know about the topic

I am going to research. Or I fastwrite a "what-I-know" draft to surprise myself.

During Writing

While I am writing the draft, I encourage the connections I do not expect by writing fast, without criticism. I continuously make use of my writer's memory, which is stimulated by the writing act, making me aware of what I didn't remember that I knew. I try not to know too well what I may write, allowing the discovery drafts to lead me. I also may make notes in the draft or on a pad of paper of things I suddenly discover in the writing: references to other writing, connections between facts or ideas, new patterns of meaning, sources I have to explore.

OBSERVATION

In the academic world, direct observation is often overlooked, yet it can be a productive source of significant information. If you are writing a paper on criminology, visit a police station or a jail; on health care, spend a few hours sitting in a hospital waiting room; on economics, walk through a supermarket or a mall; on literary studies, browse through that part of the library in which your subject is preserved; on government, attend a meeting of the school committee, town or city council.

When you observe, make notes. That activity will make you see more carefully as well as preserve what you observe. Note your first impression of a place, a book, a person. Make notes on what is and what is not; what is as you expected and what is not. Look for revealing details: how people interact, where things are placed, what is happening. Use all your senses: sight, hearing, smell, taste, touch. Take account of how you feel, react.

INTERNET

The first source for external information for many of us now is the Internet. We move the mouse and enter a universe of information. We can browse in libraries around the globe, explore other data sources, join interest groups, send out messages seeking the information we need.

The ability to use the Internet has become a basic intellectual tool essential to anyone who intends to be informed. The explosion of information in my lifetime has been a revolution of such magnitude it is hard to comprehend. When I was an undergraduate at the University of New Hampshire after World War II, we were denied a Phi Beta Kappa chapter because our library was so small. I had to go to Boston and sneak into Harvard's Widener Library to complete papers in elementary literature courses. Now, through my laptop, I have instant access to millions—perhaps billions—more pieces of information almost instantly.

INTERVIEW

Live sources should not be overlooked. If you are writing about schools, interview students present and past as well as teachers, administrators, school board members, parents. Read the books and articles about schools, but also go see the people in the classroom.

Good interviewers are good listeners. Few of us can turn away from a quiet, receptive listener who makes us an authority by asking our opinions. Try not to ask questions that can be answered with a simple "yes" or "no." Not "Will you vote to make professors sing all their lectures?" but "Why do you think it is important that professors sing their lectures?"

I like to prepare for an interview by listing the questions the reader will ask and expect to have answered. There are usually five questions—give or take one—that must be answered if the reader is to be satisfied.

"Why is tuition being doubled?"
"How will the money be spent?"
"How do you expect it to affect students?"
"What are you doing to help students who cannot pay?"

Listen to the questions and follow up on the answers to your questions: "We are raising tuition because the faculty is underpaid." "What evidence do you have that the faculty is underpaid? Can you name faculty members who have left because of pay? What positions are unfilled because the pay is so low?"

Note the answers to your questions, but check the ones you have any hesitation about or the ones that are most dramatic and surprising: "We are raising tuition so we can build the first-class Ping-Pong stadium our students demand." Journalists rarely check back with the person they interviewed, but I usually did. The purpose of the interview is not to trick the person being interviewed but to get accurate information to deliver to the reader.

LIBRARY

We live in an increasingly complex world. We need information on toxic wastes, traditions in Italian politics, Arctic survival techniques tested in Siberia and Canada, Norwegian exchange rates, the discovery of a new strain of AIDS virus in Africa and a treatment developed in Paris, the translation of the work of a Nobel Prize winner who writes in Arabic. The list goes on and on. Libraries are the intellectual closets of humankind where information is stored until we need it.

Search Techniques

Can we find the information? Not in my closet, I find myself answering. Fortunately, humankind has librarians who organize information so that it can be recovered.

Your library will be changing and increasing its access to sources of information. Go to the reference desk, but do not only ask reference librarians to help you get information on your topic; ask for instruction on how to use the library so you can do your own research. That is a skill you'll need as a lawyer, salesperson, police officer, politician, social worker, doctor, scientist, teacher, nurse, retail store manager.

The starting point for all the resources available to you—books, reference guides, monographs, articles, reports, audio- and videotapes—is your librarian. Use the librarian to learn how you can tap into the abundance of information you need to draw on to write—and think—effectively.

Effective Note Taking

It is important to have a system of note taking so that you have accurate, readable notes with the source clearly indicated.

File Cards. Most writers find that the most efficient system involves note cards—3 inches by 5, 4 by 6, or 5 by 8—on which most information can be placed, one quotation or piece of information to a card, together with the source. The cards can be easily carried to the library and ordered and reordered into categories as the research develops. It is easy to check back with cards and to line them up for reference while rewriting.

Computer Notes. More and more people are typing their notes into a computer using software programs that do a spectacular job of organizing, ordering, and reordering information.

Printout, Photocopy, Fax. The electronic world in which we live has changed the way in which we collect and take notes. I do a great deal of photocopying when I research, making sure, however, that I write on each photocopied page where it came from. I either place these notes in a file folder—with the same heading as my computer file— or type them into the computer. I also get printouts from computers or have a direct computer transfer of information into my computer files. Those are either placed in the stationary file or the computer file. Other material comes in by fax and I treat it the same way. It is vital that you know where each piece of information comes from at every stage of the research and writing process.

Creating the Bibliography

The inexperienced library researcher pounces on an enticing piece of information and forgets to note where it came from. It is useless. It is no longer a piece of important information if it cannot be cited with an accurate attribution and checked by you and a reader.

Use a system of file cards—usually organized by topic—and within that, alphabetically by author, to record the complete title of your source, the author, the publisher, the copyright or publication date, the edition, the library reference number, the page on which you found the reference. Take down all the information you or a reader may need, and record that information in the way demanded by your discipline or in a way that will best serve anyone trying to find and use that reference.

It is hard for those who have not used scholarly materials to understand the necessity of footnotes and bibliographies. It is not just to establish the authority of the writer, but to serve the reader who is doing research, to let that interested reader follow the trail of scholarship that led to your writing. It is a matter of more than etiquette. Footnote references and bibliography are a duty if you are to participate in the intellectual world, adding your knowledge to those that went before, so it is possible for those who come after to build on your contributions.

Plagiarism. Plagiarism is using someone else's ideas or writing as if they were your own. Plagiarism is theft.

But plagiarism can be avoided if the writer takes accurate notes that indicate precisely which of the author's words are being cited and which are the words of the researcher summarizing what the author said.

Of course, many students do not know the difference between quote and paraphrase. Here is the difference:

Quote is using someone else's exact words. Those words are enclosed in quotation marks: *"President Franklin Delano Roosevelt said, 'The only thing we have to fear is fear itself' in his 1933 inaugural address."* They are attributed to the person who said them by a direct attribution in the text, a footnote, or both.

Paraphrase is putting someone else's idea in your own words. *"President Franklin Delano Roosevelt spoke of the insidious effect of fear on the nation in his 1933 inaugural address."*

ATTRIBUTION

Attribution connects information with its source.

No attribution: *"Alcoholism is a problem on the campus."*
Attribution: *"Alcoholism is a problem on the campus, according to Chief Ruth Grimes of the university police."*

The reader deserves to know where the information comes from: "Who sez?" The reader ought to be skeptical, questioning the text, challenging its authority. And we have the obligation to answer that challenge.

Unstated

All the information in the draft has an attribution. That information without footnote or reference is attributed to the writer. We must remember this and make the information we use on our own authority accurate, specific, and fair.

Stated

In formal academic, research, or scholarly writing, the attribution is provided by clear statements in the draft, together with a footnote, or with a footnote alone. The footnote style may vary in a history, psychology, physics, zoology, mechanical engineering course. Make sure you know the style that each instructor expects.

Should your chosen style be less formal, it is still important to provide, in the draft itself, a reference— *"as President Bill Clinton said in his televised report to the nation on the action in Bosnia, December 20, 1994 . . ."*—that will allow the reader to look up the original document.

Reader-Granted Attribution

There is a third form of attribution, the one granted by the reader. When you write to a particular audience—police chiefs, supermarket managers, colonial historians, college undergraduates, town managers—you can refer to common experiences, express common opinions or frustrations, articulate the thoughts and feelings of your audience, and if they recognize and agree with what you are saying, that act grants you authority.

You may not have to attribute common knowledge, but you should indicate the source of any surprising or unusual information. This is a gray area, and I would lean over backward, when in doubt, to make sure your reader knows the source(s) of information central to a piece of writing that depends on research. "In 1980, only one in four college students was over 25 years old. In 1990, the proportion had nearly doubled, to four in ten," according to Sam Roberts's *Who*

We Are—A Portrait of America Based on the Latest U.S. Census (Times Books, Random House, 1994).

Discover Sources with a List

I am a great list maker, and it takes only a few minutes to brainstorm the sources that you might overlook without the list. *Try it.*

Our campus is having a problem with alcohol, and if I decide to write about it, here are a few of the sources I might use:

Students at a bar
Students not at a bar
Campus police
Town police
State police
State Liquor Commission's enforcement officers
District attorney
Judge
Campus infirmary
Local hospitals
Alcoholics Anonymous (AA)
College counselors
Local therapists
Psychology professors
Sociology professors
Bartenders
Beer and liquor stores
American Automobile Association
State motor vehicle agency
MADD—Mothers Against Drunk Driving

The list can go on. Try it. Then, of course, you have to select the sources you can contact within your time limits.

....

WRITING WITH INFORMATION

Once the writer's information inventory is full, the challenge is to use selected information gracefully and effectively. Inexperienced writers believe that effective writing is constructed with words—especially adjectives and adverbs—but experienced writers use words to communicate the information with which they have constructed their writing. John Kenneth Galbraith, the bestselling economist, explains: "I would want to tell my students of a point strongly pressed, if my memory serves, by Shaw. He once said that as he grew older, he became less and less interested in theory, more and more interested in information. The temptation in writing is just reversed. Nothing is so hard to come by as a new and interesting fact. Nothing so easy on the feet as a generalization."

THE CRAFT OF SELECTION

Writing—and every other art—involves the craft of selection. A great deal of good material, information the writer worked hard to collect, will be left out. That is the mark of a good piece of writing. And, in a sense, it is all there. The reader feels the abundance of information behind the page. The draft is not thin. It has depth and weight; it is worthy of attention.

STYLE

The style you will use to write will depend on the message or information you have to convey, the reader to whom you are writing, the occasion of writing, the publication in which the writing is to appear, the genre in which your message is carried, the voice of the draft; but there are some basic techniques to consider.

Word

The individual word carries information to the reader; and to write lively, information-laden prose we should make sure that each word carries an adequate load of information to the reader. The words that can carry the most information are nouns and verbs.

Each case depends on the situation, but consider the information contained in the simple words *house* and *home,* a choice worthy of consideration. Carry it further:

<u>She lived in a</u> house.   home.

shack.

mansion.

hovel.

palace.

tenement.

prefab.

trailer.

And look at a simple, active verb:

<u>He</u>   walks   <u>into the house</u>.

slams

strolls

darts

charges

saunters

dances

tiptoes

marches

clumps

And the list can go on. Notice how much information a noun and a verb can convey in a simple sentence:

<u>They</u>   walked   <u>into the</u>   house.

slammed   home.

<u>They</u>	strolled	<u>into the</u>	shack.
	darted		mansion.
	charged		hovel.
	sauntered		palace.
	danced		tenement.
	marched		prefab.
	clumped		trailer.

Notice how simple but different nouns and verbs change the information and the message.

Phrase

The phrase, that fragment of language less than a sentence, is often an effective way to communicate information.

He walked the streets	<u>like a soldier on patrol.</u>
	in fear of each shadow.
	as if he owned them.
	listening to his own footsteps.
	seeking the safety of shadows.
	unaware of who was following him.

Sentence

The simple sentence, as we have seen, can carry more information than we might expect, but we can load up the sentence with a great deal of information:

A university has been described, by Grayson Kirk, as a collection of colleges with a common parking problem, but I am struck, after returning to the university I attended, at how resilient an institution it is, welcoming unexpected thousands of veterans on the GI Bill after World War II and changing its curriculum, year after year, in response to society's need for study and research in many fields unheard of when I was an undergraduate: computer studies, space sciences, women's studies, black studies, environmental sciences.

Paragraph

I think of paragraphs as the trailer trucks of prose that carry a heavy load of information to the reader:

> I wonder if my post–World War II generation will be known as the generation of the single-family house. I dreamt of living in a single-family home because I was brought up in rented apartments where I was shushed by the fear that the neighbors upstairs or down might hear. Hear what? Anything. Music, fights, kitchen clatter, the Red Sox game, bedsprings, bathroom flushes, burps, curses, footsteps, doors shutting, drawers opening. And then an uncle bought a single-family home in east Milton, and I knew that was what I wanted. A house of my own, far enough from the neighbors to thump a ball, yell back, play my music at proper volume, flush the john after midnight. And I made it, one of the veterans who gloried in urban, suburban, and exurban sprawl. But my daughters, both successful, making more money than I did at their age, may never be able to afford a single-family home.

There are many other ways to carry information to the reader including illustration and graphics, but most information is communicated by word, phrase, sentence, and paragraph.

Remember that the reader is hungry for information. That is the principal reason we have readers. They want to read the specific, accurate, interesting information that will turn them into authorities on our subjects.

REVISING ACADEMIC WRITING

Academic writing has its own particular demands for information. The form of information needed depends on the discipline, even the discipline within the discipline. A paper in clinical psychology may need case histories; a paper in experimental psychology may need graphs and statistics. Effective writing in every genre—from poetry to a laboratory science report—is constructed from the information that the reader needs.

The purpose of academic writing is not just to test the student's knowledge, although that is a consideration in school. Its main purpose is to inform and to persuade, to advance our understanding of black holes in physics, to assess the importance of the new records of Lincoln's law practice in history, to have us reconsider Faulkner's novels from a feminist perspective. Our knowledge moves forward on a trail of documented evidence that can be checked by those who follow the trail of old scholarship, which is extended by new researchers and scholars.

INTERVIEW WITH A STUDENT WRITER: JENNIFER ERIN BRADLEY-SWIFT

Jennifer Bradley-Swift is a second-year student at the Residential College, an interdisciplinary college within the College of Literature, Science, and the Arts at the University of Michigan. She is concentrating in international social sciences and French, but her principal interest is photojournalism. She says, "This is my second year working as a staff photographer for *The Michigan Daily*, the student-run paper independent of the university. Because I consider the *Daily* just as much of my education here as I do my classes, I can rationalize spending upward of 25 hours a week there (making $45 a month)." She plans to spend her next two semesters studying in Paris, where she hopes to work as a photojournalist after graduation. She is also co-organizer of a project to integrate social responsibility fieldwork into the curriculum of the Residential College.

What techniques do you use to collect specific and significant information before writing a first draft?

Before writing a first draft, I start sketching (more in the form of a casual mind map than an outline) the categories of information I will need: for a paper built around a thesis, these categories are each of my supporting arguments; for research and personal pieces, they are each of the elements used to build my story. The next step is then to start the actual collection process. In any paper where I am using sources other than myself I will go through each category and pull out all of the information nuggets available—quotes or passages or facts. For most papers I collect these info-bits by copying them onto index cards: one card for each bit, complete with bibliographic info (especially page number so I can go back and remind myself of the context) so that I can easily credit my sources once I begin writing. On each card I also write my thoughts about that particular info-bit— why I think it is important for my argument, how it relates to the other bits I've collected. Using this technique, organization of the paper is simply a matter of arranging the cards. And to supplement the cards, I sometimes use a notebook on which I sketch a more fixed linear representation of the argumentative organization.

What different techniques do you use when initiating a topic or when responding to an assigned topic?

When initiating a topic, I will do preliminary info searches first to find sources and then within those sources, skimming through to get an idea if there will be enough meat with which I can create a sound and convincing argument or story. Responding to an assigned topic, I have no choice and must then do my best, finding info within the sources available for that topic; in this way I will turn more quickly to the card technique, often making notes as I read along in an assigned reading if I know beforehand what the focus of the resulting paper will be.

How do you know you need to collect more information to revise a draft?

When diagnosing problems within a draft, I look first at whether the problems arise from within the syntax and organization. I check to see if these problems are simply a matter of poorly constructed sentences that are innocently bad, or if they have the ulterior motive of trying to hide a deeper weakness within the paper. If I don't have enough information in a certain passage, I often initially try to patch the hole with redundancy and wordiness. As my mother (born an editor, I think) has taught me through years of a relentless red pen, I shouldn't use useless sentences, even the ones that may sound quite nice at first. If I'm afraid to let such a sentence go, often that fear stems from the realization that I'll have to go out once more and either collect more information or abandon my argument for lack of legitimate support.

More generally, if outside readers are not gaining the meaning—whether that meaning is an argumentative persuasion of something based more on fact, or on emotion—then either I'm simply not expressing myself well (in terms of sentence structure, expression of the information) or there aren't enough tangible info-bits for them to sink their teeth into. This can be determined by analyzing the roots of each poorly understood passage (in the manner just discussed).

What attitudes do you find helpful as you try to collect information?

When collecting information (especially when just starting), I try to remain open to all possibilities, avoiding initially discounting something that might prove useful later. This attitude is essential for me as a journalist, when both reporting and photographing. In most journalistic cases, there is no going back later to catch something I missed the first time around; if I missed it then I'm usually out of luck. Therefore, I am continually reminding and then forcing myself to ask all of the questions and take all of the pictures (from all of the angles and using all of the lenses and all of the light, shutter speed, and depth-of-field possibilities) first, and then to question, edit, and organize later. When writing papers, this means I often have index cards left over, which is a much better fate than not having enough and scrambling around when I really just want to be writing.

There are many reasons why I might be at first hesitant to take a picture: time restraints, questions of appropriateness, of being too obtrusive, that the shot will take too much energy to put together. But I never want to feel I have limited myself and my expression of the subject in question simply because I didn't take that one shot. These concerns are especially relevant when creating a photo story, a series of pictures that explains a subject through images; often that one shot becomes the foundation for the whole story.

For example, shooting the Ann Arbor Blues and Jazz Festival, I had unlimited press credentials and therefore found myself on stage with guitar great Luther Allison. During what would be the last song of his set, he switched to a cordless guitar and stepped from the tall outdoor stage to the speakers below in order to get closer to the crowd. As his guitar continued to wail the crowd wailed along with him, eating up every note. Allison then proceeded across the speakers, and was then suddenly below, with only a fence between him and the crowd. But he didn't stop there—instead he continued to walk around to past the edge of the stage and past my field of vision. Since I was still up high on the stage I wasn't sure what I should do—wait for him to return or somehow follow. While I hesitated I looked out and saw just what was happening: Allison had gone all the way around the edge of the fence and was now "in the crowd," still wailing as crazy as before. I realized there was no more time to hesitate, and if I wanted the shot I would have to act immediately. So I jumped from the stage (about 10 feet up) and ran like I have never run before—yelling and pushing my way through the crowd. With three shots left on that roll of film I got the shot—Allison lifted on the shoulders of some stranger in the controlled chaos of the moment—crowd and performer united in the appreciation of the music. It was the primary shot of the festival's photo story, and I wouldn't have felt I had done a complete job of expressing the story without it.

What specific process—or processes—do you try to collect the information?

When collecting information I most often start generally and focus down to the specifics. This means thinking about the types of sources I'll be using, finding those sources, figuring out which parts of those sources I need, and which info-bits within those parts. By *source* I mean books, periodicals, web pages, essays, class notes, interviews, conversations, memories, depending on the type of writing. In journalism, collecting information means getting background info and then going to the people most appropriate for the topic, the ones who know the most (taken from the list of those willing to talk). It means asking the right questions and being respectfully persistent in order to get the best answers. In photography, it means being able to evaluate a situation or person and trying to capture and express the right information (in the right way, considering angle, light, etc.) that will most effectively and honestly tell the story.

What tools do you use when searching for information?

When searching for information I use the actual tools of our library's computer system for book and periodical sources; the Internet is also proving very useful and if I'm not using it myself, other people are very kind to send me bits of information I might find interesting. I often use the people around me as resources. If I know someone (a professor, classmate, friend, parent) who has experience with the current task I am undertaking, he or she often has useful insight on how to get started.

When I'm reading something (either as one of several sources for a paper or a novel/play, etc., on which I'll be writing), I always read with a pen in my hand. It reminds me that I am reading for information, and that at any point of discovery I can underline or jot down a note at a moment's notice.

How do you know when you have an adequate amount of information?

I know I have an adequate amount of information when my audience gains the meaning I wished to have expressed in my paper/story/poem/photograph. Or, I should say in the case of more emotionally based pieces, when the audience has gained an equally strong (if not the same) meaning as that I am expressing.

What techniques or tricks of the photojournalism trade help you as a writer?

It is essential to be aware of the entire setting and subject matter when setting up a shoot or trying to capture the existent moment. It is an equally important thing I try to remember as I am writing. I never want to leave out an essential bit of information (an inch or two in the frame), or include too much so that it muddles the piece (photo) and the subject is lost or inaccurately portrayed. I need to have enough information about what I'm shooting (and if a photo goes along with a written article, knowing the angle taken on that article) so I can be most effective in choosing which information I will need (and in what way it should best be portrayed) for the assignment.

The difference between an assigned topic and a personally initiated one holds true for my task as a photographer at the *Daily* as it does my role as a writer: when shooting an assigned subject I must do my best to shoot what I've been assigned. But when the task is for me to come up with a feature shot (to stand on its own) or a photo story, I am responsible for making sure there is enough information available to make a good photograph, both info that makes something newsworthy and visual info that makes something a photograph.

What are the most important three things you've learned that other college writers might find helpful?

1. Never try to write something (or I should also say, defend something you've already written) when there simply isn't enough information to back it up or to give it meaning. Instead, although it will mean more work (and sometimes an element of pain), it is always worth it to find the holes and fill them instead of trying to patch them with duct tape.
2. Don't be afraid to take initiative when collecting information. Often the juiciest bits come from the hardest and most risky collection endeavors, but these are the pieces that make the story.

3. Initial steps toward organization (although they might seem silly or unnecessary at first) most often pay for themselves many times over. (Those little cards can really be a godsend.)

COMMENTARY

I have a contract with a publisher to write a book on writing as a visual art. Writers visualize when they write, seeing the subject they are writing about—the performer on stage, their grandmother in the nursing home, the reader who opposes what the writer is saying, the process of experimentation in the lab—and you should try this yourself. Most of us are familiar with the camera. We may not be photojournalists like Jennifer, but we can use our experience with still and video cameras to seek, select, focus, frame the information when we write.

CHAPTER 4

REWRITE FOR
EXTERNAL ORDER

Now that we know the dominant meaning of the draft and have collected the material from which an effective piece of writing can be built, we are ready to choose the shape or form of the building we will construct.

You, the writer, need the house of meaning as much as the reader. You have a discovery draft, a rough sketch of your writing, notes, and other research materials much like architects and contractors use blueprints. Depending on the subject, those notes—mental and physical—may include books and articles you have read, your notes on them, interviews with sources, memories, observations, lab notebook entries, historical documents, reports of experiments, draft fragments of earlier writing, government reports, scholarly monographs: in all, a total mess. Your mental work space looks like a construction site littered with kegs of nails, prefab windows, piles of lumber, shingles, tools, tar paper, concrete steps going nowhere, material filled with potential.

The writer has to control the material, to make sense of it, by shaping the information into a form that gives the material meaning and carries that meaning to the reader. In shaping the material, the writer looks to see what connects, what belongs together, what makes sense. Much of the material is interesting, but it doesn't connect with the meaning. It is placed outside the fence of form like the boards, roofing shingles, bricks, and tools that are not needed to advance the meaning are excluded from this construction site. All those that are needed to complete the building of a piece of writing that will stand on its own are included within the fence of form.

....

FORM IS MEANING

Form gives meaning to your material in the same way a house, a barn, an apartment block, a supermarket gives meaning to lumber and nails, steel beams and cement.

In writing, sometimes you can be the architect and design the building of meaning within the limitations of the material and purpose of the building; other times you are the job boss constructing the building you have been assigned from someone else's, perhaps a teacher's, blueprints. In each case, form shapes meaning.

BEWARE THE FIVE-PARAGRAPH THEME

If you have not heard of the five-paragraph theme, do not read this. Unfortunately, many of you have been exposed to the five-paragraph theme and an immediate antidote is needed.

The five-paragraph theme appears harmless. It is easy to teach and has a certain logic:

Paragraph 1: An introduction beginning with a topic sentence and thesis statement that tells the reader what you are going to say.

Paragraph 2: } The topic is defined,

Paragraph 3: } developed, qualified,

Paragraph 4: } documented.

Paragraph 5: A conclusion that tells the reader what you have said.

Sometimes a five-sentence paragraph is even required that always begins with a topic sentence and closes with a formal concluding sentence.

The teacher's intent is good: to teach form, structure, order, development. The problem is that the five-paragraph theme lives only in the classroom. It is not written or read outside of school.

Today's reader is impatient. The reader wants the writer to get to the subject immediately. The topic sentence is rarely used, and the same thing is true of the conclusion. Once the writer has said what is to be said, the writer gets offstage and does not turn around and tell the reader what it means, how the reader should think or feel. It is too late. And few subjects can be deposed of in three paragraphs—it takes the time it takes—one paragraph or 25, half a page or 100 pages.

The five-paragraph theme has dangerous implications that reside like a computer virus in the student's brain:

- The form of the draft is more important than the content.
- Meaning can be changed to fit the form.
- There is one right way to tell all stories.
- The reader has to be told what the message will be, what the message is, what it means.

Effective writing grows organically: the form comes from the meaning. You may have to fit an imposed meaning—the company demands that all accident reports be written exactly the same way—but if you are reporting a hazardous situation and there is not a required form, then you can study the information and the person for whom it must be created and organize it so it delivers what the reader needs. The corporation lawyer may need to be aware of potential lawsuits, the personal director of the danger to workers, the production manager, the loss of production. The form grows organically, naturally, from the message and its intended audience.

THE UNSHAPED MATERIAL

The writing demonstration that follows is constructed from the facts: the writer's parents divorced and his father got married soon afterward. His mother had just remarried the summer before the writer left for college. This is a good piece of writing that dramatizes a situation faced by many young people. I am impressed at how compassionate the student is and how little he wallows in self-pity. He does not judge his parents and he has a sense of humor. The shape of the piece is clear: a paragraph for each situation in chronological order. The purpose is to look at an autobiographical situation critically. It is a critical essay in the sense that he shows how his parents—all four—change and behave as they take on new roles.

The form doesn't quite work at the end as he lumps in all the other family he has grown in the last few years. This draft could be developed in the first paragraph, or it could be developed into a longer section or even an essay of its own.

In the beginning I had two parents, then I had three, now I have four. In editing my last paper, the instructor said that "less is more." Well, in remarriage, more is more. Lots more.

I didn't realize when my father moved out how much he would change—and how much our relationship would change. At first he was just angry; then he became like a buddy. He grew young. We hung out on visiting days at McDonald's, the mall, ball games, watching TV in his small apartment. He told me his troubles—me!—and asked me for advice. And he listened to me and seemed to understand the way he never did when he was my father. Well, he was still my father, sort of.

Mother changed. She became SUPERPARENT. She read books and went to meetings and even signed up to coach my soccer team—and she was good. Read books on that too. When she and Dad were together, she was the easy one. Now she was Ms. Boss—and at work too, where she got promoted. My father grew young; my mom grew old. Not ancient, just responsible, organized. She became an executive mother. She gives me memos on what to do—on office forms!

Then Dad married a woman who made cookies. She made like she was a Disney mother. Annie, she wanted me to use her first name, cooked whole sit-down, cloth napkin meals. She gave up her job because she was pregnant. Well, I had stayed over in that small apartment on the living room sofa before they were married. A baby was no surprise to me. It was for them! And I've become her maternity project. It was OK and I like the kid. But it was weird at times, to have a second mother and my not-real one being in a motherly phase.

Now Mom has remarried and I have an extra father. I thought if my mother remarried, I'd have some awkward guy like my friends do, who tries to kid around, be a pal, like my father before he had someone else to date. Not this guy. He had six kids before his wife died. He is in charge, and I think Mother likes that. He makes charts. We have chores. We eat around a dinner table, all of us. We have topics at dinner and I thought I would hate that, but it's fun. He really wants to be a father.

And not only do I have four parents and eight grandparents all living, and three great-grandparents, I, an only child four years ago, have three brothers and four sisters. I cannot count the cousins and the aunts and the uncles. I even have a brother-in-law.

Now see what happens as he tells his story in a different form.

SCHOLARSHIP APPLICATION

I am submitting this application to the Hogue Student Foundation because my family's financial situation has changed since I last applied. My father has remarried and he has a new baby; my mother has remarried and I suddenly have seven siblings on that side of the family, only one who is old enough to have gone to college. I hope you will consider the changed status of my two families in considering this application for a scholarship.

LETTER TO A FRIEND WHO IS IN THE SERVICE

You talk about barracks life. Well, Mother married Mr. Fertile. I have ten people wanting in the bathroom at 7 AM. I shower at school after practice. They're OK I guess but no privacy. I know what you mean about being alone. I never liked being alone, but now I have bunk beds and 7-year-old twins in my bedroom. I can't wait to go back to college and that dorm I complained about last year.

BOOK REPORT

In his book, *Role Seeking: The Sociology of Rank-Ordered Adolescents in the Extended Family,* Dr. Finley Robespierre of the Mescowan Family Research Center puts the experience of many college freshmen in a social context. At first I felt cheated of my individuality to discover I was part of a familial trend, but it was illuminating to find out that . . .

NEWS REPORT

More than 50 students attended an organizational meeting of Students of Divorce at the Memorial Student Union Monday evening.

Marianne Morison of the University Counseling Service introduced Penelope Stearns-Upton, who is both the daughter of divorced parents and a single mother, and a graduate student doing a doctoral study on the effect of divorce on freshmen.

Her pilot study revealed . . .

CASE HISTORY

Subject: Myles J. Turner, 18 years old, is a freshman from San Diego, who received word of his parents' separation in the third week of the semester.

Method: The subject was interviewed once a week during the rest of the first semester. The interviews lasted from 1 to 2 hours and took place in his dormitory room. They were tape-recorded.

His parents and siblings, a sister who is in law school in New York City and brother who is married and works as an insurance salesman, were interviewed by telephone and taped with their permission. All of his teachers this semester, the dorm resident supervisor and his hall resident, his roommate, his girlfriend, herself a child of divorce, and three close friends were also interviewed at least twice during the semester and the books and articles on the attached reading list were studied.

Discussion: The subject passed through anger, self-blame, and a beginning of acceptance during this first semester. He was able to articulate the stages through which he was passing and that concerned him, "My Dad always had a certain detachment that I didn't like. Every time I screwed up he asked, 'Now what have we learned from this?' I'd like it better if he just got pissed off. I worry I'm standing back from my feelings the same way, that I'm him."

We could go on to imagine a term paper, a letter to a grandparent who is worried about him, the minutes of a meeting of Students of Divorce, a personal journal entry, a political science paper on the legal rights of children of divorce, a scene for screenwriting class, and on and on. Each form would make its own demands because it is designed to achieve a particular purpose and serve a particular reader.

....

DIAGNOSIS: INEFFECTIVE FORM

The purpose of all written forms is to carry meaning to a reader. The form you choose must fit the material you have collected and the audience who will read your piece. The form you choose depends on the expectations of the reader. Those who give grants expect a proposal; the literature teacher expects a critical essay; the laboratory assistant, a lab report; the history teacher, a research paper; the judge, a lawyer's brief; the bereaved parent, a letter of sympathy.

The ineffective form is one that does not deliver the information the reader needs—the poem sent in as a scholarship application, the personal letter written in the style of a sociological paper. Scan your draft, imagining it as a blueprint of the exterior walls of a building. Does the shape of the building fit its purpose? Is it a factory, a summer home, an apartment house, a supermarket, a medical clinic, a fire station? Is it an argument, a narrative, a case history, a report, a poem, a review, a lab report, a critical essay?

Turn yourself into the reader of your draft. Does the material fit the tradition—the reader's expectation—or break the tradition and increase its effectiveness? Would you, as a reader, respond the way the writer expects you to respond? Is this the most effective way to attract and hold the reader's attention?

Does your draft, for example, follow the "building code" of an argument? Does it define and clarify the key issue? Does it make your position clear? Does it anticipate and respond to the opposition's arguments? Does it place your own arguments in increasing order of importance? Is each argument supported with objective documentation? Is the source of each piece of documentation available to the reader?

Such questions are obvious for each form. Imagine you are the reader, and list the questions that must be answered by the shape of your draft and the information delivered within that shape. Your account of an automobile accident can be shaped by the task: filling out an insurance report, dictating your account to the police, giving a lawyer material for a brief, preparing a eulogy for a victim's funeral, writing a letter of sympathy to a parent or a personal letter to a close friend.

In scanning your draft, determine whether the form is appropriate. Does what you have to say fit the tradition, the form the reader expects? Many times in school or work, of course, the form is ordered ahead of the material: it will be a term paper, a corporate memo, an argument, a case history. Then the focus will be on collecting the material that will satisfy the form.

If the form of the draft is appropriate to the material and to the audience, then you can move ahead to the next stage in the rewriting process. If not, then you may have to choose a different form, turning a report into an argument, an argument into a personal essay.

When the form is required by an instructor or an employer, the writer can only adjust the form—switching the point of view, reordering the evidence, casting the traditional form in a manner more appropriate to the message being delivered. Even when you cannot choose the form, you can still make it yours by the way you develop it.

....

FORM COMMUNICATES MEANING

The form of what we say contains and therefore helps to communicate our meaning. A house invites us to live in it; a field house invites play, a factory invites productivity. *Story* says there is a beginning, a middle, and an end; action between people shapes events. *Essay* states there is significant information worth critical commentary. *Lyric poem* implies there is truth to be found in image and song. *Description* declares there is something important to describe; *report,* that something has occurred that needs to be reported to a reader; *argument,* that there is something to be argued for or against.

....

DISCOVERING THE FORM OF THE DRAFT

To build a house of meaning, a structure that delivers significant information and a critical opinion of that information, you have to choose an effective form. Just as each type of building has a different purpose and a specific structure to serve its purpose, so does each form of writing.

INTERNAL FORM

Most writers try to find the form within the draft. They read the draft to see how the information they are collecting dictates the content:

The writer discovers:	*the possible form*
a significant pattern in ordinary information that the reader needs to understand.	expository essay
significance revealed by a series of events organized chronologically.	narrative
facts that contradict a law or regulation.	argument
a situation that needs study.	grant proposal
a book that readers need to discover.	book report
an individual who has made important changes in the way we live.	biographical profile
a personal experience that will give the reader helpful information.	autobiographical essay
solution to a problem at work.	memo

In the cases just listed, the form may not be clear until the writer has completed a discovery draft. The writer may begin thinking that the material will become an autobiographical essay and it may turn into an argument or a memo; the student may begin to write an argument and discover that the material demands a humorous memoir.

I respect my material and listen to it for what shape it seems to be developing. A writer should respect the integrity of the specific pieces of information collected, especially if those details contradict what the writer expected; a writer should respect the patterns into which this material arranges itself—meaning that arises from the material—especially if it is traitorous to the writer's intent. A writer should respect the message from the language—the music of the evolving text, its voice—especially if does not say what the writer thought it would say or was saying during the writing of the draft. It is the material, in the best writing, that determines the form.

EXTERNAL FORM

Of course, much of our writing must fit an external form that is established by tradition or reader expectation. We are not allowed to look into our material to find an essay, story, poem, history, research paper but must fit our material to an assigned form such as a lab report, corporate memo, critical essay, history term paper.

In these cases we follow the tradition. We manipulate the form we are given so that it delivers a meaning to a reader. We can, and should, be given a model to follow when we are assigned a form that is new to us. If we aren't, we can ask the teacher or the employer for an example or look one up. We may, to our surprise, discover we know more about the form than we realized. That conscious seeking of tradition will connect with the subconscious knowledge of which we are not aware.

Tradition

When facing a writing task you have not attempted before, find out what forms have been successful in the past by looking at books that analyze and explain argument, business writing, screenwriting, science writing, writing for nursing and police reports, newswriting, fiction and poetry writing, scholarly writing, writing criticism and speeches. Such books conduct autopsies of successful writing in that form, revealing the conventions, the tricks of the trade, that have worked in the past.

It is also possible to take a piece of writing you like—or one the audience you are trying to reach trusts and respects—and analyze to see what the author has done. Let me give you an immediate example of writing and rewriting from my own professional experience. Many high schools are returning to a system of tracking students that I hated when I was in high school. We were given intelligence tests and placed in tracks from one to thirteen—one was honor college-bound students; thirteeen was male shop. I wanted to point out that, in fact, we were tracked by the economic, social, ethnic status of our homes and forced into ghettos.

> Looking back, I realize with horror how tracking affected our lives out of school. We were separated—tracked—from junior high on: college track students never attended class with business students. They never went to class with home ec and shop students. When the economic differences were reinforced by dividing the classes by I.Q.—10-1, 10-2, 10-3 in college and then all the way down to track 13 "general" who were expected to drop out anyway—we hung out with people in our own track. We dressed according to track. I could tell a 1 or 4 or 8 or 13 track student by how they dressed, the slang they used, the jokes, each level's protective snobbery. Our parties often seemed tracked.

This paragraph is from a column I wrote arguing against tracking in school because of the effect it has on students, citing my own negative experiences with tracking. The paragraph worked and was published. But in analyzing it, I realize I could put it in a larger social context.

> When I go back to my hometown I am struck at how accurately the program that tracked us into college, secretarial, commercial, vocational, and general classes predicted what we would be decades later. The program even predicted an amazing number of our dating and marriage patterns. I wonder what would have happened had we not been tracked. Would the factory worker have become the doctor, the doctor the druggist, the engineer the car mechanic, the housewife the lawyer, the judge the housewife? Did some test, full of racial/gender/ethnic/economic bias,

predict our lives because we accepted the school's evaluation of our worth as our own?

No magic. Just a careful reading of a draft, asking what the writer is doing, paragraph by paragraph. An effective piece of writing, one that works, will stand up to this type of scrutiny and instruct a writer who needs to understand the form.

Reader Expectation

The experienced writer anticipates the reader's expectations and makes use of them, developing, pacing, and voicing the draft to the reader's desires. If the boss wants specific facts, the writer delivers specific facts; if the reader expects understanding, the writer understands; if the company president will only consider an argument that appeals to the brain, the writer serves up thought; if the reader wants emotion, the writer provides emotional material; if the reader is busy, the writer is brief.

The writer becomes the reader, imagines what the reader expects, and delivers in many forms of writing. Each form the writer uses has its own pattern of reader expectation, and since we are readers as well as writers, we can predict those expectations.

Writing Against Expectation

Some of the most effective writing, however, is written against the reader's expectations. The reader expects a sermon and receives a humorous story; the reader expects humor and receives a government report filled with facts that the reader slowly discovers is hilarious; the reader expects an emotional argument and is delivered a list of hard, cold facts; the audience expects a high-flown political speech full of grand clichés and hears a quiet, honest piece of autobiography; the reader of an annual report expects statistics and is taken on a walk through a manufacturing plant.

You can work against reader expectation when the draft communicates significant information in the manner most appropriate to that information; but it is important, in some way, that you let the reader know that you know the reader's expectations and are contradicting them on purpose.

Or you may be able to accomplish this more subtly, but readers who come to the page with an expectation—and all readers do—deserve a response to their expectation. If you don't anticipate their expectation, they will go away early and go away mad, and you aren't an effective writer if your readers leave and don't turn the page.

DESIGN YOUR OWN FORM

One of the delights of writing is to design your own form that carries your individual information to your own reader. Many writing tasks do not fit a traditional form or they combine traditional forms: description and argument, book review and essay, narrative and memo. The experienced writer soon learns to design a form that fits the task.

THE DISCOVERED FORM

To discover the organic or natural form that lies within a draft, read the draft quickly, trying to visualize the outlines of the piece, its horizons or boundary fences. There may be several forms in a draft. It may tell a story and use narrative techniques; try to persuade the reader and use some of the strategies of argument; relate facts in a manner appropriate to a scientific report. All these techniques might be used in a magazine article on an environmental problem. But the overall form would be an investigative piece of magazine journalism. Your job is to discover the form that contains and communicates the message effectively.

THE INVENTED FORM

The invented form is created from the three principal elements:

message
purpose
reader

Once those elements are identified, the process of invention is usually a matter of simple logic. At first the inexperienced writer writes drafts and eventually discovers the need to invent a form to do the job; the experienced writer sees the need ahead of time, but the process of design is the same.

Message

What is said comes first. The message itself, "I need money," is a force in determining the form. Each message may need a special container that will carry it efficiently to the reader.

Purpose

The purpose of the writer is another force that shapes form. The purpose of the message, "I need money," may be to get sympathy from a friend, to delay a suit from someone to whom you owe money, to make someone pay up who owes you money, or to negotiate a loan from a parent, bank, or college financial aid officer.

Reader

The one who is to receive the message also exerts a profound influence on the form. An appeal that works with a mother may not work with a father. A friend who owes you money may not be influenced by your good grades, but a financial aid officer may be affected by that information.

CREATE AN EFFECTIVE DESIGN

It is a simple, logical matter to create an effective design, a rhetorical form that is custom made to communicate a message to a listener and accomplish a clear purpose. Remember, you have been using speech to persuade, report, entertain, communicate since before you started school. You know many of the forms of our literary heritage, you simply don't know the names that scholars use to describe them, and that doesn't matter in the designing process.

Put the following headings across the top of a sheet or pad of paper, even at the top of your computer display screen.

Message ———▶ Purpose ———▶ FORM ◀——— Reader

Write a brief description of your message in the left-hand column; add a statement of purpose in the second column; then jump over FORM and write a brief description of your reader. Now consider the forms that might deliver that message to that reader and accomplish your purpose. It may be the form you have used in the first draft, the form you used with some modifications, or a form you have read and written before. It may also be a way—new to you—of delivering a message to a reader.

Here are some examples of how this method might work.

Message ———▶	*Purpose* ———▶	*FORM* ———▶	*Reader*
I have two years' experience waiting on tables, one cooking.	to get better summer job.	• Letter saying how much you love Rock Beach, how much fun you had there as a kid.	Ms. Gates—owner.
Want job as summer night-shift manager.		• Letter telling how much college costs. • Copy of short story about funny things that happened where you worked last summer. • Letter describing experience in businesslike terms, including references and plans to go into hotel management. • Memo based on observations as a customer making specific suggestions about what night manager should do to increase customer satisfaction and profits. Add a brief résumé.	Tough, suspicious of college kids.

No mystery here. Read the proposed forms from the point of view of the employer. The last one gets the job.

Try this yourself on a proposal to change your major, get academic credit for running a duck farm in the summer, use military credits for your major, apply for a student loan. The creation of an effective form is a matter of logic.

USING A TRADITIONAL FORM

The forms you invent are usually on the shelf in the rhetorician's warehouse. They may be under general headings such as narrative, argument, report, or they may be categorized by purpose: to persuade, to tell a story, to explain, or to instruct. The forms may also be in a specialized warehouse: chemistry lab experiment, sales report, U.S. Army training manual, history term paper, nursing log, engineering field journal.

In whatever field you study, there will be forms that you can try on for size, adapt, and modify to fit your message, purpose, and reader. As you write, you will develop the inventory of forms with which you are familiar, but never forget that you can invent the forms you need when you face a new writing task.

....

KEEPING IN, CUTTING OUT

The effective writer creates from an abundance of information, an abundance of thought, an abundance of feeling. The experienced writer feels the same panic in facing this abundance as the inexperienced writer, but the experienced writer knows that the feeling of going down for the third time under the ocean of information, ideas, and emotions is natural and essential. Effective writing is the product of a full inventory of material from which the writer can choose to construct a sturdy piece of prose. The writer has to be able to pick the appropriate quotation, the revealing detail, the precise word, the supporting melody, the accurate insight, the fitting feeling, the documenting statistic, from a warehouse of potential material. And, therefore, the revising writer has to master this abundance, making effective use of what is on hand to discover, clarify, and communicate meaning.

WHAT IS SAVED

All that is saved in the draft is the material that gives the form shape and meaning. Each detail, each word, phrase, line, paragraph must move the meaning forward. When revising, the writer must, with a cold eye and an icy heart, examine each piece of information the writer has collected, each lovely phrase the writer has created, and save only those that clarify, develop, support, communicate the meaning.

WHAT IS DISCARDED

Consider writer Isaac Bashevis Singer's wastebasket. He said, "The main rule of a writer is never to pity your manuscript. If you see something is no good, throw it away and begin again. A lot of writers have failed because they have too much pity. They have already worked so much, they cannot just throw it away. But I say that the wastepaper basket is a writer's best friend. My wastepaper basket is on a steady diet."

What is thrown into the wastebasket is not wasted. The material not used—that fascinating specific, the unexpected quote, the phrase that once seemed to illuminate, the concept that once appeared to bring all the elements together—led to what was used and what is in the process of revealing meaning, as well as what will be shared in the final draft.

Go through a draft and make a plus mark in the margin opposite what must be kept and a minus mark opposite what might be cut. Cut and see if the draft becomes stronger. Usually it does, partly because you have the space to make the best parts better.

REVISING ACADEMIC WRITING

The challenge of academic writing is to find a way *within* the tradition to express your own critical views, to be individual within formal limitations. To do that you have to first conform to the limitations. In addition to the suggestions just made, many disciplines, through their formal academic organizations or the publications of those organizations, publish guidelines for published research. These can be obtained from a professor or by writing the organizations. A reference librarian can also show you a directory for such organizations.

Once you are familiar with the writing expected in a field, you can adapt those traditions to the needs of your material. All forms of writing, even academic forms, evolve in response to the latest trends in research. Composition research traditions have changed, for example, as researchers study students in the context of their lives in and out of school. Most disciplines have changed as computers have become a basic research tool. In revising an academic paper, it is vital to know the traditions of the particular form your writing must meet.

INTERVIEW WITH A PROFESSIONAL WRITER: DONALD M. MURRAY

Evelynne Kramer, who was then my editor at the *Boston Globe,* asked me to write a piece of personal experience about a summer place or event that was important to me. I immediately thought of writing how I learned to swim, since I almost drowned twice before learning to swim. I saw the piece as a straight, chronological narrative.

> July. Bright sun glints off blue lake water. Water splash and each drop a bright crystal of light. Rocks rising at the shore where sun-laden maple leaves make leaf shadows dance. Dark pine woods, cool and mysterious.
>
> Swimming underwater where the temperature drops and sunlight dims. Flipping over to study the ceiling of water overhead. Joy and terror.
>
> It was in July that I drowned. Twice.
>
> And it was in July that I learned to swim.
>
> The first time I drowned was at Salem Willows. Mother was laughing with some lady friends at the bottom of the pier and I was at the far end, reaching for a rowboat when a boy in the next boat, laughing, shoved my boat away with his oar and I fell into the water. I could not swim.

I still dream the crusted pilings racing up, the water turning green then black, the unexpected cold.

I came to on the dock, hands pushing at my back, water spewing from my mouth, and Mother running toward me. I did not know mothers could run.

The next time I drowned was at Ocean Park in Maine when a Baptist minister was hired to cure the scaredy-cat little boy of his fear of the water. His was a muscular, male Christianity.

He grabbed me and swam me to the middle of the salt ocean pool where the water was over our heads and tossed me, arcing high in the sky, to where the water was even deeper.

I splashed my way back to him and got him around the neck. I was not holding on. I was determined to kill him for his betrayal—and I almost did.

I remember my thin arms under his chin as I hugged his neck—hard. I remember our going down together, bobbing up, going down again; I remember the glee I felt as I saw his face, close up, go red then dark, anger changing to terror.

He fought me to the edge of the pool where Christians rescued him. I was punished and ridiculed all summer, but I felt enormous satisfaction. I did not go in the water again that July; I did not learn to swim.

And every time I saw him in the pulpit, at the camp, on the sidewalk, I reveled in the look of pure Christian hate and fear he sent me.

It was another summer that I was sent to Camp Morgan, a Worcester YMCA camp in Washington, New Hampshire—a skinny, lonely, only child my uncles felt was spoiled. Camp would make me a man: I would learn to swim.

I was to spend four summers at Camp Morgan, nine weeks each July and August, and my personal geography will always include the Millen Lake, the stumble-rooted trails in the woods, the chapel I helped build, Half-Mile Point, the ball field, Blueberry Hill, a thousand overlapping summer scenes.

I can still feel my legs pushing up Chocorua, the pack high on my back; watch rain create craters in blueberry pancake dough cooking in a frying pan over a smoky, open fire; experience a gentle ride in a canoe and its response to the soft turn of my trailing paddle; discover once more the cellar holes of towns abandoned in the gold rush; wince at the painful surprise of a bee that stung a boy's most private part as he sunbathed on an Asheulot River rock after skinny dipping.

And each July I remember the terror of swimming class, the cruel taunts of instructors and campers, the humiliation of hiding in the woods or crouching in the stinking KYBO [Keep Your Bowels Open] hearing the cheers and laughter, the instructors' whistles and the campers' splashes, and the shouted "Murray" by the counselor assigned to find me and drag me back to the lake.

Shame and ridicule and cruelty at last made me more terrified of not swimming than of water over my head. Day after day, the last boy to swim, I got in the water up to my ankles, then to my knees, then bent over and got my face in the water, at last learned to keep myself moving where I could touch bottom and, weeks later, found myself leaping into water over my head and swimming—but never to this day without fear.

A former teacher, I do not today approve the methods used to teach me to swim. My instructors seemed unnecessarily cruel, gloating at their ability to humiliate. This system did not work for everyone. Some left camp and went home, but camp, even under these conditions, was a happier place for me than home, and I was Scots stubborn. I stuck it out.

After Camp Morgan, paratroop training in a hot southern summer not so many years later was a lark. And when I was in combat I often remembered that July when I was more terrified of retreat than moving further out into water over my head.

Ever since that July 60 years ago when I first drowned, I still fear the terror of water over my head, and when I swim, I slowly move out further and further, my feet touching bottom, then my toes, then nothing.

Once I am in water over my head, my fear under control, I am free to ride the surface of the water, then to dive deep, swimming underwater, slowly turning so I can see the ceiling of water, sunlight refracted by water, remembering the old lessons and remaining calm, not fighting the water, enjoying the beauty of the water world.

It was in November that I had my heart attack, but as they worked over me in intensive care, it was again July, at Camp

Morgan, and I repeated the lessons I learned there: to survive, accept this changing world, do not waste your strength in struggle and splash; focus on staying afloat.

The nurses congratulated me on my attitude, not knowing I was once again learning to swim. Following the lessons of July, I made it to shore again, and in the unexpected life that follows I also remember the July lesson to enjoy the beauty of the world.

The terror of drowning—of aging, of leaving this summer world—is still with me, but it is under control. And the terror makes the fragile beauty of water spray against the sun, the pattern of leaf shadow, the mystery of dark pine woods, more beautiful each July.

After lunch Evelynne called to say she had reservations about the duly learning-to-swim feature. I offered to dump it; but she said it could run, though she thought it could be better.

She thought it took a long time to get into it. I suggested that place was at paragraph 17. She thought it was further down, four paragraphs from the end!

More notes I made while she was on the phone:

- gets good as it gets rolling
- long time to get to meaning
- lot of time spent introducing characters not significant to me
- perhaps rethink the narrative
- get to the point about death, fear, heavy-duty stuff

I was fascinated by her comment that the piece started four paragraphs from the bottom, and that starting at that point would change the piece from a narrative into an essay reflecting on a series of experiences. I started at the end, rewriting by working within the draft to see what this new form would tell me.

The following draft is shorter, tighter, more immediate. You may find it interesting and instructive to take your draft as I am going to take mine, and go through it paragraph by paragraph to see just what I have done in the revision. It can also be helpful to do this to a piece of writing you like.

It is again July, and I stand in water up to my chest. I try to talk away the fear of my drownings, fail and suddenly make myself spring up and then down, swimming underwater, out where my feet cannot touch bottom.

> *Remember: What I say in this commentary is spoken by the editing me who must be rational and objective about what the writer me did instinctively. Now I stand at a distance and rationalize what I did when I was unconsciously instructed by the draft and my craft.*
>
> *I want to put the reader into my shoes—oops, bare feet—so the reader can experience my fear and my response to it. I also want to establish the tension that will drive my piece: my fear of swimming and my delight in swimming.*
>
> *I hope for reader identification, that readers will begin to experience their own Julys as they read mine.*
>
> *And a hint of something mysterious—"my drownings"— that may make the reader read on. Also an echo to that moment of terror we all felt when our "feet cannot touch bottom."*
>
> *And all in 42 words.*

The water is cold, dark as I remember and then I swim up to light, break the surface and tread water, my fear under control until another summer.

> *I get the reader in the water.*

July is always a month of joy and terror, the month I twice drowned, the month I learned to swim.

> *This is the context paragraph, the place where the personal experience essay to be told is placed in a larger focus. The reader is promised, by implication, that the individual experience will have a significance that goes beyond its importance to the narrator.*
>
> *I develop the tension, working from specific, physical details to more psychological issues. I look back to the paragraph, fourth from the end, of my first draft, to see how I took off from there. In a way writing is like jazz improvisation, picking up a theme and, within a tradition, running with it.*

Now I am free once more to enter the water life pool, river pond, ocean. I ride the surface, jackknife and dive deep again, swim underwater—my greatest joy—slowly turning so I can see the ceiling of water, sunlight refracted by water remembering the old lessons and remaining calm, not fighting the water enjoying the beauty of the water world.

> *I want to share my celebration of swimming with the reader. I did not realize the importance of "remembering the old lessons and remaining calm, not fighting the water" when I first wrote it, but it now foreshadows what will come in the piece and will be repeated in slightly different words in the third paragraph from the end. Those words contain the ultimate meaning of my essay; but I did not know that when I wrote them here and I did not remember these words when I wrote them at the end of the piece. I feel as if this meaning was discovered and woven through the piece by the draft. My job is to read and follow the evolving draft—the evolving thinking that is writing.*

I suppose the terror of drowning—of aging, of leaving this summer world—makes the fragile beauty of water spray against the sun, the pattern of leaf shadow, the mystery of dark pine woods, more beautiful each July.

> *Now I echo back to my first "poetic" beginning as well as to the terror and deepen the feeling in the piece that is, in a way, about dying. I see that now, but didn't know it while writing drafts. The themes of writing come from the writing, rarely before. Once more I am aware that writing is thinking, not previous thinking written out.*

The first time I drowned was at Salem Willows; I was 8 years old. Mother was laughing with some lady friends at the foot of the pier and I was at the far end, reaching for a rowboat when a boy in the next boat, laughing, shoved my boat away with his oar and I fell into the water. I could not swim.

> *Now I am back to the chronology but I move faster than I did before. I have a complicated series of actions to make clear. To do that, I see the scene with memory's eye and record what I see—in sequence.*

> *The point of greatest impact or emphasis comes at the end of a paragraph—or a sentence or a piece of writing. Short sentences also give emphasis. Note my short sentence at the end of this paragraph.*

I still dream about the crusted pilings racing up, the water turning green then black, the unexpected cold.

> *I want to put the reader in the water, drowning. Note the action: what's going up fast means I'm going down fast; the color of the water, then its temperature.*

I came to on the dock, hands pushing at my back, water spewing from my mouth, and Mother running toward me. I did not know mothers could run.

> *A touch of humor at the end of the paragraph to lighten the seriousness of the experience. Of course I didn't think that and put it in. And writing this I realize the humor is black. I was surprised that my mother was so concerned about me, perhaps a cruel and unfair thought but a true one. I wrote it because that was what I remembered as I recreated the experience in my mind and on paper. In rewriting, I cut, save, or develop, rationalizing what I wrote instinctively.*

Each July, when I dive down into the cold water below the surface, I see those pilings rushing up.

> *I connect past and present.*

The next time I drowned was at Ocean Park in Maine when a Baptist minister was hired, a couple of summers later, to cure the scaredy-cat little boy of his fear of the water. Ours was a muscular, male Christianity.

> *In writing the first draft, I discovered I am still, perhaps even more, angry with that minister now than I was when I was a boy and subjected to the behavior of grown-ups. John Hawkes says, "Fiction is an act of revenge." Perhaps, in part, all writing is an act of revenge, a very uncomfortable thought.*

He grabbed me and swam me to the middle of the salt ocean pool where the water was over our heads, and tossed me, arcing high in the sky, to where the water was even deeper.

I hope the reader is in the air with me.

I splashed my way back to him and got him around the neck. I was not holding on. I was determined to kill him for his betrayal—and I almost did.

I remember my thin arms under his chin as I hugged his neck—hard. I remember our going down together bobbing up, going down again; I remember the glee I felt as I saw his face, close up, go red then dark, anger changing to terror.

He fought me to the edge of the pool, where Christians rescued him.

A series of very complicated actions to make clear and some not so complicated emotions to reveal. Revenge? Well, I guess so. Glee—just the right word. I cut out the external comments about teaching philosophy and methodology from the previous draft. Show and there may be no need to tell.

He taught me what I did not know: there was a man inside of me, a tough, cold man of rage that I met years later when I served in combat as a paratrooper.

But I do need to put the experience in a larger context right now. What did it mean to me, and perhaps to my readers? What did I learn and what might my readers learn? Too often personal experience pieces remain in the personal; their significance is not revealed. This is not just the story of a spiteful kid, no matter how justified. It did mark me in a way I—and the reader—do not expect but understand once it is said.

When I finally learned to swim at Camp Morgan, the Worcester YMCA Camp then at Washington, New Hampshire, the mechanics of the crawl, breathing to the side, the overarm stroke, the flutter kick were easy. It was the fear that was hard.

More context and the specific details give it authority and make the writing lively. We write with specific information.

At first I would not go to swimming class, finding my fear of water greater than the taunts of instructors and campers, the humiliation of hiding in the woods or crouching in the stinking KYBO [Keep Your Bowels Open] as the counselor assigned to hunt me down shouted "Murray" until he found me and dragged me to the lake.

Now I can begin to create the climate of counterfear, of ridicule and shame, that made it worse for me not to swim than to swim.

At last I learned to jam the fear down inside me, to control the shaking, the tears, the cramps in my gut, and to dare the water, at first up to my ankles, then my knees, at last, weeks later, over my head.

On this reading, I think I hear the reader asking, "How did you control the fears?" I stop right now and create a new paragraph. But when Evelynne edited the story she had problems with the paragraph that piled up like a train wreck. I agreed. Too much, too much.

I quickly rewrote the paragraph three times, making it tighter, cleaner. Evelynne liked the result.

(Original) I learned how we control fear intellectually, observing that others can swim, others that are often more inept than I am; I learned how we control fear physically by taking deep breaths, forcing our muscles to relax; I learned how we control fear socially by being more afraid of not doing what others do than of doing it; and I learned, most of all, to abandon myself to terror giving up hope and diving in.

(1st rewrite) I learned how we control fear intellectually, observing that [added] others who had knees that drummed against each other, lips that trembled yet moved further and further out into the lake [cut] ~~still can swim, others that are often more inept than I am~~; I learned how we control fear physically by taking deep breaths, forcing our muscles to relax; I learned how we control fear socially by being more afraid of not doing what others do than of doing it; and I learned, most of all, to abandon myself to terror giving up hope and diving in.

(2nd rewrite) I learned how to control fear by mobilizing the fear of not measuring up to counterattack the original fear taking a deep breath, abandoning myself to terror and diving in.

(3rd rewrite) I learned how to mobilize the fear of not doing against the original fear of doing and, in that moment of calm, take a deep breath, abandon all hope, and dive in.

Now, in this crucial paragraph the reader demands are clear as I use small words in a direct manner. I worried about the echo of the reference, "Abandon hope, all ye . . ." and decided it would work for people who did not get the reference and enrich the text for those who did.

After Camp Morgan, paratroop training in a hot southern summer not so many years later was easy—well, relatively easy. And when I was in combat, I often remembered the July when I had to dive into water over my head.

This continues to reveal the significance of what I learned at summer camp. I also hope the reader will feel again the childhood terror of water over your head so they will accept the larger terror that follows. Now I am coming to the end—and the full meaning of the piece.

In the November I had my heart attack I silently repeated the lessons I learned at Camp Morgan: Do not waste your strength in struggle and splash, but accept the world you fear; relax and float on the unknown.

What I learned is spelled out in a still larger, more immediate context. The reader may apply these lessons to the reader's own experience.

Remember what I wrote in the fourth paragraph.

During the attack and afterward the nurses congratulated me on my attitude, not knowing I was once again learning to swim.

Busy, busy, tying all the threads of the essay together.

Each July in the unexpected life that followed, I stand in water, then force myself to jackknife up, then dive down, turn, rise easily to the surface, float on what I fear, grateful for yet another July.

"Float on what I fear." Yeah! Go get 'em, Murray.

And a return to the joy of swimming now experienced in depth—pun intended. The essay on learning to swim becomes an essay on learning to live while dying as we all are. The reader will not articulate that, but many will feel it and be moved by it as they relive their own living in the face of death.

Did I know it meant that? No. Not when I wrote it. Not when I revised and edited it. Not when I read it in the paper. The writer often is the first and last reader; the writer writes and rewrites to discover what the writer has to say. The surprise of what I have to say that I did not know I had to say is what draws me to my writing and rewriting desk every morning: I thought I was writing about learning to swim.

Shaping our drafts becomes one of the writer's great delights. We all write against chaos, trying to understand the confusion of life. By leaving some material out, including other material, ordering it, discovering patterns, we begin to see meaning. As we continue to shape the material during the process of revision, meaning becomes increasingly clear—to ourselves and to our readers.

CHAPTER 5

REWRITE FOR
INTERNAL ORDER

Readers should be drawn into a piece of writing so they will follow a trail that leads to meaning. The writer must create a path of continual seduction that keeps readers interested and eventually satisfies them.

Readers are in control. Readers can leave the writing at any time and will if they don't have a sense of progress. They may not be told explicitly where the writing is taking them, but they need to have a sense that they are moving toward meaning.

Rewriting effectively means reading what you have written with a stranger's eyes to see if there is a clear, seductive trail of exploration that runs through the draft. That line may be clearly marked by headings or it may be hidden within the material, but readers must sense a sequential order in what they are reading or they will put the writing down.

DIAGNOSIS: DISORDER

In diagnosing a draft, there may be many signs of disorder. For example, the writer may start out describing the drinking policy on campus, then suddenly switch into the history of fraternities and sororities and antidiscrimination laws, return to the drinking policy, then go into the author's own high school drinking history and swerve back to the college alcohol regulations. The reader loses track of the topic and the writer's opinion, and stops reading. Disorder is not attractive in a kitchen, but it's fatal on the page. Here are some of the signs of disorder in a draft:

1. The trail through the draft is based on a sequence of false assumptions or assumptions that are true only to you, the writer. Count the false assumptions in the following example. I count three whoppers.

Example:

We should not send good tax dollars to foreign countries. Other countries do not have the moral standards of the United States. Better to use those bucks at home, in our cities, for example, where people cheat welfare but at least it is on the economy like at least if you make a bad loan it should be to someone in the family, then there's no trouble.

2. The writer tells us the emotions the writer wants us to feel, but we need less emotional direction and more details that make us feel for both people. The reader should have the emotions; the writer should inspire those emotions from what is written on the page.

Example:

I was so overwhelmed when I saw my father, after all this time, and in a hospital bed. It was so sad, I almost cried. In fact, I did cry, the hospital bed and everything. I remembered him young and he was so suddenly old. All the feelings of hatred and resentment and anger and loss surged up within me. And yet he was my father. It was tragic, so sad for him and for me.

3. The draft was written by a kangaroo who takes great leaps for reasons the reader does not understand.

Example:

If we are going to do something about the deficit we should start by paying ball players less. The owners of professional teams make money so do universities from football but the workers earn more than is appropriate in a nation that has a foreign trade imbalance and a national debt to reduce. Taxes on sport tickets might help.

4. The writer is lost in the accumulation of information that seems to have no context, no fascination for anyone but the writer, no order.

Example:

I have put a new Pentium 120 chip Lexus 480M but I don't need to in my laptop, new, that already has a Pentium 133, with lotsa ram—32 mg—and even with memMaker and Qemm, I get General Protection Faults but that's probably my scanner or Omnipage if it isn't my 4 quad CD-ROM, but the Zip drive is great.

5. The writer wanders off the trail to examine wildflowers, butterflies, and mountain streams that are interesting but have nothing to do with the subject at hand.

Example:

Trust is the most important element in a relationship. I certainly discovered that after the accident in the sculpture studio last week when my roommate trusted her partner and lost three fingers to a power saw a classmate said he knew how to operate. I wonder the role of trust when people perform dangerous jobs in the military, as lumberjacks or as farm workers, especially children.

6. The rewriter asks, "How does this piece of information advance the reader's understanding of the subject?" and finds there is no answer.

Example:

Automobile manufacturers have adapted vehicles to the needs of their customers and to the dreams of their customers they may live in an urban area but they like to drive adventure vehicles, four-wheel drive and all, as if they were pioneers. These vehicles allow the driver to sit up high and they are ready to ford rivers, up canyon arroyos, whatever, drive through snowdrifts in the Sunbelt.

7. The sequence is unnatural, because the reader has to leap back and forth in time or logic for no artistic reason, going from A to F to C to G to K to B.

Example:

There are things I know now about college sports recruiting that I didn't when I needed to. I can't blame my parents. They never went to college, to high school. What my high school coach told me was all wrong. I can't believe what he said. And it wasn't just this school. I was made promises like you can't imagine. And no one told me what would happen to me if what happened happened. Now I know and it's too late. But maybe the appeal will help.

8. The draft reads like Swiss cheese, it is full of holes.

Example:

The latest treatment for diabetes, at least in tests, is far better than current practice and will be appropriate for all kinds of diabetes although the treatment will differ unless new technology is developed, as has been announced, and its cost is cheaper than what patients have to pay now, a substantial figure at best.

9. The reader's questions are not answered the moment they are asked. The effective writer can predict when the reader needs a definition, documentation, an example, more description by hearing the reader's subconscious questions: What's that word mean? How come? Who says? So what?

Example:

"Wysiwyg" made it much easier for me to write textbooks a computer generation ago. Of course that was always true for Macs, but I have had to live in the DOS world and that limited me until I moved to WordPerfect 6.0 and chose graphics mode, but now I am beyond that with Windows 95 and Word where wysi-wyg is page layout—what's next?

....

ANSWER THE READER'S QUESTIONS

I have found one organizational technique more effective than any other in revision: anticipate and answer the reader's questions. Any piece of writing is a conversation with a reader who interrupts to say:

"How come?"

"How do you know that?"

"Says who?"

"I don't get it."

"What do you mean?"

"I'd like to know more about *that*."

"No kidding."

"Why'd she do that?"

"What'd he do then?"

"Tell me more."

"Stop it. Enough already."

"Get to the point."

"Whoa. Back up, I don't understand."

"Whatta you mean 'gaseous diffusion'?"

Inexperienced writers—and some experienced ones—do not hear that half of the conversation. All effective writers hear the reader's questions and *answer them the moment they are asked*. In an essay on civil rights, here are the questions the reader might ask about your draft:

- Who is most responsible for the passage of the Civil Rights Act of 1964?

- Who was for it? Against it? Why?
- What federal civil rights laws—if any—were in place before the Civil Rights Act of 1964?
- What did it accomplish?
- Why was it needed?
- What did the law say?

I usually find that there are four to six questions that *must* be answered to satisfy the reader. They are the simple, obvious questions that someone who is deeply involved in the subject may forget, but the common reader will ask. They may even be questions the writer does not want to have asked, but there is no escape: those questions will be asked.

After the writer has determined the questions, the order in which they will be asked can be anticipated. The question third from the end in my example should be last and the one second from the end should be first (and the third question can be incorporated into it).

- Why was the Civil Rights Act of 1964 necessary; weren't there laws against discrimination?
- Who is most responsible for the passage of the Civil Rights Act of 1964?
- Who was for it? Against it? Why?
- What did the act provide?
- What did it accomplish?

Can you use this technique *before* you write the first draft? Of course. I still have to use it in revising and in editing other people's copy. A version of this that I have used in revision is to write the reader's questions which the writer is answering in the margin of the draft and then reorder the piece to anticipate the sequence in which the reader would ask them.

....

OUTLINE AFTER WRITING

I have emphasized outlining as a rewriting or planning activity, and of course it can be. But to do an effective outline in advance of writing, the writer has to have a firm idea of what the draft is going to say. And many times, since writing is thinking, it is impossible to write anything but a brief sketch outline ahead of time, or if it is written ahead of time it bears little resemblance to the first draft.

But it is always helpful to outline during revision to reveal the structure of a draft, and then to design the structure that the draft must have to satisfy the reader.

TO EXPOSE THE STRUCTURE OF A DRAFT

Here are some of the ways the writer can strip away the language from the draft and reveal the structure underneath:

- Ask the reader's questions as described earlier.
- Read through the draft and make a formal outline to visualize the structure of the draft.
- Use the movie writer's storyboard and put each topic you come to on a slip of paper with a reference to the page and line in the draft (statistics on rural poverty p. 3, l. 13–22). Then rearrange the slips of paper into a logical sequence.
- Create a computer tree or draw one that shows the sequence of major points in the draft in the way that computer programs display directories and subdirectories.
- Draw a graph with a computer program or on graph paper that shows how the major issues rise, fall, and interact with other issues in the draft as graphs show the rise and fall of the stock market.
- Write a quick, shopping-list sketch of the main points in the draft.
- Make a computer printout of the draft on your screen; underline or otherwise mark the key phrases; then cut away the rest of the draft to see the structure revealed.

- Write out the questions asked by each section, and then look to see if they are answered in the following section.
- Write down the major section headings to see the line—the logical order—that is the skeleton of the draft.

ADAPT THE STRUCTURE

Once you see the structure of the draft, you can often imagine the structure the reader needs. It may be easy to adapt your draft to the needs of the reader by moving sections around, perhaps creating new ones and eliminating old ones. Such moves may be suggested by test readers—classmates, workshop members, instructors, editors, friends, family—who, because of their need to understand and their distance from the writing of the draft, see a potential new structure clearly.

REDESIGN THE STRUCTURE

Many times the structure of the draft has to be abandoned; it just doesn't do the job of producing a draft that can be understood by the reader. In this case you have to design a new trail through the material.

This is a good time to work backward:

- Write down at the bottom of a page what you want the reader to think and feel after reading your draft.
- Pick a starting point in the material that is as close to the end as possible while including all the information the reader needs to arrive at the conclusion you have written down at the bottom of the page.
- Note the three to five pieces of information the reader needs, in sequence, to arrive at your ending.

Of course, you can design an outline with the reader's questions or with the other forms of outlining described on page 221.

....

REVISING ACADEMIC WRITING

Order is of enormous importance in academic writing, which is always concerned with critical thought and an orderly, intellectual movement from point to point. Some disciplines have formal orders that should be followed, unless it is necessary to design a new order to communicate your meaning. But, to be honest, few academicians will allow beginners to do that. Find out if your instructor or editor has a structure you must follow in writing a laboratory experiment, a business or sociological case history, a book review.

....

INTERVIEW WITH A STUDENT WRITER: KATHRYN S. EVANS

Kasey Evans is a 20-year-old English major and a junior at Princeton University. She graduated from Oyster River High School in Durham, New Hampshire, where she received the Yale Book Award, the Valedictory Medal, the faculty Honor Key Award, the Robert Byrd Scholarship, a National Merit Scholarship, and several departmental awards.

With a grant from the Princeton Plasma Physics Lab, Kasey held a 1995 summer internship, teaching math, science, and English to middle school students from the Trenton public school system. In the summer of 1996, she worked as an intern in the production department of Heinemann Books in Portsmouth, New Hampshire, and hopes to continue working as a freelance editor for Heinemann during the year.

At Princeton, where she has studied under Russell Banks and Joyce Carol Oates, Kasey is the editor in chief of *The Princeton Eclectic,* a writing magazine for which she has also served as contributor, copyeditor, and fiction editor.

What techniques do you use to plan or outline information before writing a first draft? How do you adapt it during the research, drafting, or rewriting process?

Prewriting—in both the amount I do and the strategies I use—depends on the kind of writing I'm doing. I begin essays by writing stream-of-consciousness notes. I start with obvious citations, or a rehashing of class discussions, and free-associate. Certain ideas or themes reappear. I connect these with arrows, or asterisks, and continue writing about how or why the two instances of the idea connect.

Why does Dante use the same phrase to describe himself, at the beginning of the poem, and the false prophets down in lower Hell? Plato's idea that we are all degenerate versions of a single perfection— why does that same idea appear in Boethius? And then again in Augustine? And then Milton, and then Faulkner, and then . . .

These notes aren't in full sentences, and end up looking like annotated road maps. Once I think my road map contains enough information to complete the assignment, I start to translate it into an outline. I write an approximate thesis idea at the top of a clean sheet of paper. This thesis—which usually lacks a verb, and so is still mostly a vague idea that will, hopefully, give rise to a thesis—names what the arrows stood for in the map: "Dante's anxiety about his own sin" or "degeneracy: human life as turning away from the 'real.'" (The would-be thesis usually sounds pretty incoherent at this point—it's not just that I've given poor examples.)

Then I start to list the passages or quotations that started me on my road mapping in the first place, trying to group them into some kind of order. After I write each quote/idea, I write how that evidence relates to the idea at the top of the page. I'm still thinking at this point, not just reorganizing; I'm still trying to make connections that will flesh out a thesis.

By the time I've slogged through the instances that I included on the road map, along with any others I've thought of while writing, a theme has hopefully developed, one that will supply a verb to that thesis idea at the top of the paper. Then I can go back and revise that heading:

"Dante's anxiety about his own writing makes him feel sympathy for the false prophets."

If I feel confident about this outline, I'll start drafting on the computer from the notes that I have. If the connections still seem tenuous, if I'm not sure that my evidence really says what I want to make it say, then I go through again, making more notes, drawing more arrows, revising the thesis, until I have a more secure outline.

The fiction writing that I've done hasn't required similarly formal prewriting. I carry a daybook/journal in which I write down the stuff of my day: bits of dialogue, anecdotes, descriptions, topic ideas, smells, and anything else that seems as if it could provide fodder for later writing.

Because the assignments I've had for fiction classes are permissive (i.e., "write something this week"), I don't plan so much as I plunge. If I begin with a voice of a character I think I want to use, I'll write in the first person for a while and see what comes of it. If I liked the girl behind the counter at the coffee shop, then I'll write a scene about what she did when she got off work and see where it goes.

When writing fiction, I use the drafting process to discover my story and to surprise myself. I'm not willing to be surprised by my essays, for the most part (especially when I'm writing them at three o'clock in the morning of the deadline, as I am wont to do). If I haven't learned something in the process of writing the essay, then I have written a terrible essay. The things that I learn in the process of writing essays, though, work within the structure that I have planned for them. The things I learn when writing fiction are more drastic: that character isn't actually his sister; she's his girlfriend, and she can't appear until the fourth chapter.

This discrepancy means that I rewrite most of the fiction that I draft, and I merely revise the essays.

How do you know you need to revise and switch to a different tactic or reorganize a draft?

I need to reorganize when there's nothing to say. If I find myself avoiding a piece, or starting 17 new stories so I don't have to go back to an ongoing one, I can be pretty sure that I need to make substantial changes in the draft that will make it appealing again.

The most common substantial change I make in fiction pieces is a voice change. I get bored if I'm in first person and want to know what the other characters are thinking, but can't; I get lost and overwhelmed if I'm in third person, trying to understand how all 37 characters understood their night at the beach when Bob is the only one who seems to be having an interesting night. Voice change is also a somewhat safe place to start reordering a draft, because it doesn't require that I give up the entire premise of a story. I don't have to admit to myself, "Well, maybe this one isn't going to work." (At least, I don't have to admit it yet.) I can keep the concept, keep the dialogue, keep the setting: I just have to rethink the way I go about telling it.

What attitudes do you find helpful as you order your raw materials or reorder a draft and what specific process—or processes—do you use to reorder a draft?

The most difficult, and the most important, thing for me to remember when revising is to be willing to abandon what I've done. I try to rehearse in my head: "You are capable of writing well. To say that, however, does not mean that just because you have written it, it is written well." I think often of Ann Lamott, in *Bird by Bird,* when she wrote about an editor who rejected a novel she had written. "Your problem," he told her, "is that you think that everything that has happened to you is interesting." Not everything, I remind myself, is interesting just because it comes from your brain.

As a guideline, to keep myself from becoming too wedded to my first drafts, I try to cut at least a third of what I've written. I literally take a word count, and cut until a third of that number is gone. This sounds arbitrary and silly, but I've never had to cut any keystones. The way I draft, I can easily cut a third of my first-draft words without losing the heart of a story.

To lessen the pain of making major cuts, I keep a document on my computer entitled (strangely enough) "cuts." When I start to agonize about whether to cut a paragraph/page/section/dialogue/description, I cut it and paste it into the document. Pasting it somewhere makes me feel as if I haven't completely abandoned it, and makes me less reluctant to cut. (I have never, incidentally, pulled anything back out of the "cuts" document and reused it.)

I try also to remember that the stories have all been told before. I'm never going to entirely create something—I'm just going to inherit a story that's already been told about 100 times (99 of which told the story better than I will). People have told me that they think this is a cynical attitude for a writer to adopt. I disagree. If the stories have been told before, then what I am doing is proposing that I have something to lend to them. I have a voice, or the capacity to adopt a voice, that no one else could give to those stories. I have confidence that my voice and my vision are a valuable asset to hundreds of years of telling the same story.

This attitude is a helpful one to keep in mind when revising because it keeps me honest, and (hopefully) unpretentious. "Kasey," it reminds me, "you don't have anything new to say. You aren't going to create anything new today. So why don't you just relax? Why don't you just say what you mean, and say it the way you mean it? Why don't you stop using big words and images that don't make any sense? Why don't you just say what you mean in the best way that you know how? Because that's what you have to offer—a vision of something that 100,000 people in the world have already seen. Have faith that your vision is worth telling, and tell it with clarity."

How do you know when you have completed the reordering process?

I don't.

I'm not trying to be facetious, but I've never finished a story. I cannot read anything that I've written without cringing and wishing that I'd revised it 75 more times before I let anyone read it.

I think, though, that at some point I have to agree to let things go. I have to agree to let the piece be imperfect and to start something new. When I'm rewriting or revising, I am learning new things about my characters. It's obvious in the drafting process that writers learn what their characters do. In most interviews, or books on writing, that I've read, authors say that their characters surprise them all the time. If their characters don't surprise them (look at that! she's leaving her husband to run away with that single mother from the day-care center! and you didn't even know!), then the characters aren't real, the story is dead, and the writing is worthless.

For me, this process of discovery continues all the way through revision. I cut that section, and reread, and all of a sudden I know what goes in place of the section I cut: the waitress has to go find that guy who left the $100 on the table instead of a ten (look at that! and I didn't even know!). Once this process of discovery is dead, and the changes I'm making during revision aren't teaching me anything new about the characters, then it's time to let go.

What are the most important three things you've learned that other college writers might find helpful?

1. Be honest. Don't say things you don't feel or don't understand. Your dishonesty will show. Writing dishonestly won't make you feel good about your writing, either—won't make you feel compelled to go back to the piece.
2. Be willing to let go of what you write. Don't hold drafts as sacred. Don't be afraid of destroying and rebuilding.
3. Write every day.

COMMENTARY

None of us get to college without experience in spoken and written language. Sit down and list what you know about ordering a piece of writing. Then think of the jobs you have held and the other subjects you have studied. List the ways of ordering material in those worlds that may apply to writing. Finally, create ways of ordering material that might work. Make a file: All I Know About Organizing a Piece of Writing.

You will discover how much you know and realize you have a method of discovering how much you know that can help you to face a "new" writing problem that isn't new after all.

CHAPTER 6

REWRITE TO DEVELOP

The most critical difference between poor, unread writing and fine, well-read writing is development. People imagine that a creative idea—the more eccentric the more creative—is what marks good writing. But there are few if any new ideas. The creativity and the quality comes in the development of a piece of writing.

Fine writing makes the writer's vision of an idea, a place, a person, an event clear to the reader with a rich blend of revealing specific details, observations, references, patterns of thought—all the forms of information appropriate to the subject.

It is also the richness and fullness of the text that gives the writer authority and makes the reader trust the writer. Joseph Conrad said, "My task . . . is, by the power of the written word, to make you hear, to make you feel—it is, before all, to make you see." The writer recreates experience—with texture and in depth—so that the reader sees, feels, thinks.

DIAGNOSIS: SUPERFICIAL

Undeveloped writing is difficult for the writer to diagnose because the draft is fully developed in the writer's mind: it just isn't on paper.

The writer writes, *"it was a terrible accident"* and sees the victims trapped in the car, hears their cries for help, hears the sirens, is bathed in the flashing light, sees the rescue workers using the jaws of life, sees the blood, the body rushed to the ambulance, bottles with intravenous tubes held high, sees the next victim wheeled slowly to the next ambulance, a blanket over the head. The writer has only delivered a blank check = *"terrible"* to the reader.

Another writer says it is *"a good idea to raise gasoline taxes"* but the reader asks, "Why?" and finds no answer in the text. An intern writing a marketing memo says, *"there are obvious markets other than youthful ones that CompuGames should exploit,"* but she does not go on to identify the markets and how they could be reached.

Those readers will not read on. The writer has to develop the ability to stand back and create a distance between writer and draft so the writer can read the draft as the reader—hungry for information—will read it.

The signs of an undeveloped draft are many: it is predictable, it could have been written by anyone, or a computer, there is no individual vision; the draft lacks an abundance of revealing details; it is full of generalizations with no documentation. The draft is not satisfying to read; the reader learns nothing the reader did not know.

Take a piece of your writing and write *more* in the margin wherever you would like more information. Do the same with published and unpublished writing you like and do not like to see how a well-developed piece of writing serves you and an undeveloped one does not.

....

TECHNIQUES OF DEVELOPMENT

An effective piece of writing has depth that goes below the surface and a richness of texture that attracts and holds the reader. *"We suffered a flood"* becomes *"I expected a huge, sudden tidal wave, wind, rain, but what we experienced was worse, the quiet arrival of the river that usually was a mile away, first a trickle, then streams and puddles, then the quiet, continuous rising of water as far as I could see, my horizon rising and trees, telephone poles, houses, barns all sinking out of sight, quietly, certainly."*

Three basic problems with many early drafts can be solved by development: there is little information, the reader doesn't know if the information is authoritative, and it is not clear what it means. Solving these problems, however, does more than satisfy the reader, it educates the writer.

DEVELOP WITH INFORMATION

Never underestimate readers' hunger for information: specific, accurate, lively information that informs readers and allows them to inform those around them. Readers want to gossip, to pass on information they have just learned.

Reveal with Specifics

The writers we read, enjoy, trust, the writers who inform and stimulate us, write with information. Nonwriters think they write with words, brightly colored balloons empty of information, but words have no value unless they are loaded with information. Words are nothing in themselves. They are devices to carry information, the way a check is a device to deposit, withdraw, or transfer money in the bank. No money, the check bounces; no information, language bounces.

An empty paragraph: *"Newspaper editors are masters at displaying what has occurred so that readers will know what has occurred that should, or may be, of interest to them so they can increase their stored information."*

A full paragraph: *"Newspaper editors take thousands of stories every night and display them so the reader can see their significance instantly. Page-1 news is the most important news and the most important stories are at the top of the page with the largest headline. The most important single story is in column 1 at the right-hand side of the page. Then the editors break the stories down by section: foreign, U.S., local [metro], home, business, sports, using the same top of the page and right-hand column 1 to indicate the stories that readers should consider reading."*

Write with Abundance

Meaning, form, order, voice lie within the material. Developing a draft is an intellectual act of enormous importance. We don't think or write with telegraphic summations— *"environment should be saved"*— but with a rich plenitude of information about a specific threat to the wetlands and the details of complex problems that might result from a specific solution.

Here's an example of a developed paragraph on the topic just mentioned: *"Building a dam solves the flooding problem that can damage or destroy the important wetlands, but the dam is, of course, a permanent flood that causes damage upstream, burying important biological features underwater and changing the patterns of wildlife above the dam forever."*

DEVELOP WITH AUTHORITY

"Who sez?" is one of the most significant questions academic and other readers ask. Readers should not believe the writer is the authority on everything in an article or book. The reader will demand that the writer attribute significant pieces of information to an authoritative source.

Convince with Authority

It is specifics that give the writer authority with readers. Readers are impressed by an abundance of information that convinces them the writer knows what he or she is talking about. Instead of *"Mozart composed a great deal of music,"* I might write, *"When I feel in need of a symphony I choose the Linz by Mozart; when I'm in a piano concerto mood, I reach for the 15th or 16th by Mozart; if an opera is in order it will probably be 'Cosi Fan Tutte' by Mozart; a string quartet, one of the Haydn Quartets by Mozart; a piano trio, by Mozart; clarinet or bassoon or French horn or flute or organ, it will be Mozart."* The reader should say, "He knows his Mozart."

Persuade with Evidence

Most writing is argument. We want to persuade the reader that our vision of the world is true, the reader should share our opinion, follow our leadership, vote for our proposal, buy our product. To persuade the reader, the writer must deliver evidence that the reader will believe.

Personal Documentation. Some of the evidence may be personal. In writing about date rape, a student could describe what happened to her roommate, a friend from home, a sister, herself. The reader needs to know where the documentation is coming from. *Attribution* is vital in persuading the reader, who should be suspicious of information that is not connected to an authoritative source. For example, *"I know. I went out in college with a guy I'd known since sixth grade and was raped."*

Objective Documentation. Most evidence comes from impersonal sources. The reader of the article on date rape demands—fairly or not—to know if this is a problem of that particular writer or if it is a widespread problem. For example, *"The Atwater Report of 1996 documented that date rape occurs on this campus, in our dormitories and our fraternities as well as in off-campus housing."*

The writer should build her case with an abundance of information that comes from campus and local police reports, medical records, campus housing administrators, sociological studies, case histories of victims. Again, attribution is vital. The reader needs to know from statements within the text or footnotes where the writer has gotten the documentation.

DEVELOP WITH CLARITY

What we write is often correct, but the reader doesn't get it because it is not clear. We need to develop our drafts so the meaning is not only clear to us but to a skeptical reader.

Description

Description is the mother of all writing. With words we describe our worlds, physical and intellectual. We describe observations, ideas, theories, people, events, concepts, experiments, emotions, processes—the range of human experience. Two essential elements of effective description often forgotten by inexperienced writers include dominant impression and natural order.

Dominant Impression. The description has a focus, and everything in the description supports a single impression or meaning.

Everything in the operating room was sharp: piercing light glinted off stainless steel equipment with clean edges; the sounds of machines echoed brightly off the tile walls; the eyes of masked doctors, nurses, and technicians probed the patient; a tray held a battalion of knives, each sharpened, pointed, waiting.

Natural Order. The reader should receive the description in a natural order, a story built on chronology, time passing; a description of an argument moving from the weakest to the strong points; a place seen in the order the narrator would see it.

The first thing she felt as they wheeled her into the operating room was the sharp piercing light that glinted off stainless steel equipment. Then she became aware of the clean, precise edges of the equipment, the clatter of tools and the pulsing beat of the machines that would breathe for her, the piercing eyes of masked doctors, nurses, and technicians, and before the mask came over her face, a glimpse of a tray with a battalion of knives, each sharpened, pointed, waiting.

PUT MEANING IN CONTEXT

Many writers deliver information—facts, quotations, case histories, reports—that are interesting but cause the reader to ask, "So what?" Pure information is not enough; that information has to be put in context. The anecdote or personal experience must be in a larger context for the reader to understand its full meaning.

For example, consider an interesting bit of information without context: *"The homicide detective said, 'We always start at the same place: the victim knew the person who killed him.'"*

Now, with context added: *"During my research into the causes of murder, I talked to a homicide detective who told me, 'We always start at the same place: the victim knew the person who killed him.' I added 'or her' and realized that murder was an intimate crime. I had to move in closer, escape the charts and statistics, and talk to murderers and the families of their victims to understand the causes—and effects—of murder."*

Since it is easier to see what someone else's writing needs than your own, take a piece of writing by another writer on a subject you know well, and mark in the margin how each paragraph or section that needs it could be developed.

....

REWRITING STARTS
WITH REREADING

The writer first has to reread to see what is on the draft's page, what is not, what should be. Reading for rewriting demands some very special reading skills.

READ FRAGMENTS

Often potential meanings are hidden in a word, a phrase, a line. I have had to teach myself to read fragments, and so should you. When we read our drafts we are like the archaeologist who finds a fragment of a bowl, the preserved ashes of a fire, a sharpened piece of stone, and then uses a trained imagination to create a civilization.

Many forms of fragments reveal meaning. Here are some that I frequently discover.

Code Words

These are words that have a private meaning for us. I read "basement," an ordinary word, and suddenly remember that was the word in first grade which took on a new meaning and a terrifying, seductive mystery. When I went to first grade the basement was where you were sent when you raised your hand and said, "I have to go," and it was where other little boys told you . . .

Revealing Detail

When I had my heart bypass, I was part of a machine for 91 minutes. That we can survive while surgeons manipulate such a vital organ as a heart opens the door to the poems and columns I have written about that experience. That revealing detail could lead, in my hands, to a novel; in another writer's hands to a screenplay, a nonfiction book on heart surgery, a play, a biography of a surgeon, or an autobiography of the patient.

Significant Phrase

In New England, we all look forward to *Indian summer,* those days in the late fall when the weather suddenly turns warm. But the phrase was born in fear. In colonial times, the pioneer farmers worked their fields with musket nearby and huddled at night in crowded forts where they could protect their families against attack by Indians. When it started to get cold, the Indians would not attack and the families could live in their homes beside their fields. Then the weather would change and the Indians would return, surprising individual families. That phrase has for me two hidden meanings, meanings that have a tension filled with possibility for writing.

Haunting Image

After we buried my father, I went into my parents' bedroom and found my mother sitting alone on the edge of their double bed that had been worn to the shape of their double forms. I am haunted by that image. We all have those snapshots of memory that carry enormous loads of meaning we may choose to explore and share by writing.

....

READ WHAT ISN'T WRITTEN

I think it is important to read positively, to recognize the potential within the draft, but there are drafts in which no potential is apparent. It is neither on the page nor in the world from which the draft was written. Beginning writers must read to see what is not even in the rough draft. Drafts without apparent potential usually display some or all of these deficits.

PROBLEM: NO TERRITORY

The writer has not created a world of people, events, or ideas the reader and the writer need or want to explore together. An inviting world has a richness and a complexity that interest the reader.

> *Before:* Often the U.S. Supreme Court has to rule on ethical as well as legal issues.

SOLUTION

Move the location of your article to a place where you are familiar enough to know the simplicities and the complications that interact to make good writing. A paper on ethics might be moved from the Supreme Court, where you haven't served, to the football field, where the coach has just asked you to cheat by faking an injury. On the other hand, it is equally possible to write about faking an injury in the context of National Collegiate Athletic Association rules, emphasizing research rather than personal experience.

> *After:* I am only able to go to college because I have a football scholarship but I'm not a star. I'm special teams on kickoffs and punt returns; I hold the ball for the place kickers; I carry the ball in certain short yardage situations; and, although we are a religious school, I am the quarterback's retaliator and the guy who fakes an injury on the coach's command.

PROBLEM: NO SURPRISE

The reader reads only what the reader expects. The reader knows what is coming next. There is no challenge, nothing that provokes a thoughtful or an emotional reaction from the reader. There is no suspense.

> *Before:* Research into the nation's early history may change the contextual environment of our mythic beliefs.

SOLUTION

Look over your notes, written and mental, to see what surprises you, what you learn, what you question, what your reader needs to know, what runs against expectation, to find a subject that will interest a reader.

> *After:* We think of "Indian summer" as a delightful return to summer in the autumn before winter sets in, but the term had a different context in colonial times. Then settlers feared the unexpected warmth because Indians, who did not attack in cold weather, suddenly returned to raid isolated farms.

PROBLEM: NO WRITER

The reader does not sense the presence of a human being behind the draft. The draft does not breathe; there is no individuality. There is none of the essential human music we call voice that is essential to the individual act of one person, a writer, meeting another person, a reader, on the page.

Before: One is rather overwhelmed when one arrives on a university campus from a small community for the first time.

SOLUTION

Read the draft aloud and tune it until you find a voice that sounds like you and is appropriate to the meaning of what you have to say. This may mean writing in the first person—I—or in the third person—he or she. Whoever the speaker, the reader needs to sense a single human intelligence behind the words on the page.

After: I chose this university because I came from Eagle Pass, population 105, and was graduated second in a class of seventeen in a county high school. I wanted to escape. I knew everyone and everyone knew me. Watch out when your dream comes true. Here I know no one and no one knows me. I'm doing solitary.

PROBLEM: NO RESPECT

The writer does not respect the subject matter, the reader, or him- or herself. The writing task is not taken seriously, but kissed off, dependent on superficial tricks that call attention to themselves, not to the subject. The writing cheats the reader. It is dishonest.

Before: In an election year, politicians talk of entitlements, but nothing is ever done to cut off these payoffs to freeloaders.

SOLUTION

You are revealed when you do not take the subject seriously. Find a topic that you can take seriously and write with your heart as well as your head. Look for a way to respect your topic, to have compassion for the people involved, to respect opinions you may not share.

After: I know there is welfare fraud, but last weekend we put my grandfather in a nursing home. He worked hard all his life, voted Republican, even refused his veteran's bonus after his war, but the care he needs costs $3,500 a week, without extras. He worked as a truck driver. Now his bill will be $182,000. He needs Medicare, Medicaid, Social Security, anything he can get.

PROBLEM: TOO LITTLE

The reader is given nothing but generalities. There is no information, just emotional or intellectual generalities that pass over the surface of the subject. There is no evidence that allows me to think with the writer. There are no revealing, resonating details.

Before: New zoning regulations may be needed in a college town, but they should not be aimed at students.

SOLUTION

We often feel that writing is most intellectual when it is full of generalities, but theories must arise from fact. Readers are hungry for an abundance of accurate, specific information that allows them to do their own thinking.

After: Zoning regulations in a college town should not be aimed at students but at behavior—the number of people who live in an apartment or a house, the number of cars parked outside, the noise made by boom boxes, the activities that are lumped under the term "party." The people whose behavior upsets the neighbors may be students or not. The target is not any group of people but the actions of people that affect those within eyeshot or earshot.

PROBLEM: TOO MUCH

The writer floods the reader with too much information of equal importance, or pours so much rhetoric on the page that the reader drowns in language.

Before: The party started early, before the football game, at lunch, with beer and then the guys got booze into the game in hip flasks and then we all went out to the lake where Flynns serves the best steaks but it was crowded and we had to wait an hour and a half in the bar, where, of course, there were girls and they'd had a few. We did eat lots of peanuts and I saw my priest there but I don't think he saw me. He was pretty red-faced. Well, that's not the point. The point is that Rafe outdrank us all. He always did and there was no talking him out of driving, never is. Two dead.

SOLUTION

Whether you are writing a term paper, an essay, or a story, be careful not to load up on so much specific information that the hearing of each piece is lost and your writing becomes a jumble of unrelated information. Decide on your single, dominant message and then cut anything that doesn't move it toward the reader.

> *After:* Saturday I lived a TV commercial against drinking and driving. We drank from 11:30 in the morning until 10:45 at night when the police, the wreckers, and the ambulances arrived at the intersection. Two stretchers left with the sheet over the faces of two of my best friends.

PROBLEM: TOO PRIVATE

The writer is so close to the subject that the reader has no idea what the writer is talking about. The writer produces a mumbling monologue of code words and phrases that may mean something to the writer but are obscure to the reader. Private writing is a particular problem when the writer becomes, at least in the writer's own mind, an expert on a subject, such as the Internet, honeybees, systems engineering, the history of the Dred Scott case.

> *Before:* When I added a 120 Pentium I could boot my computer and get a GPF faster than ever before.

SOLUTION

Put your writing in context. This can be done with a short paragraph, sometimes with a sentence, sometimes with a phrase.

> *After:* When I turned on my computer with a new, far speedier chip, I found that I could get to a problem message telling me I

had a memory problem faster than ever before. I had not solved the problem. I had just gotten to it faster.

PROBLEM: TOO PUBLIC

The reader is embarrassed by the writer who tells readers more than they want to know about the subject, often providing an excess of inappropriate, intimate details that do not seem to relate to the topic.

Before: My husband wanted sex before breakfast every day. He'd been so sweet before we were married and I like spontaneity, but not the same spontaneity every day, after jogging in the afternoon, Friday and Saturday night after parties, especially when we visited home and my parents were in the next room. Him on top, me on top, in the shower, in the car, all the strange stuff. He had a book and it was like we were taking a course, chapter by chapter.

SOLUTION

It may help to write about the subject in the third person, combining personal documentation with more objective sources, standing back just a bit from the subject.

After: She didn't think her marriage could be saved because her husband who had been her colleague at work saw her only as a sex servant after marriage, but couples therapy helped him see how she felt, and they worked it out.

PROBLEM: NO SIGNIFICANCE

The information the writer provides is not put in perspective. There is no emphasis, no clear point. The writer is just delivering information. There is no evidence the writer has thought critically about the subject and what it means.

Before: A foxhole in infantry combat holds just one person. Close together, makes you vulnerable to mortars, hand grenades, mines. Extended order means you march with several yards between you. Taking cover from each other, you disappear from your own army. Greater firepower means a single soldier can command a large field of fire.

SOLUTION

Writing is always a form of critical thinking. The reader expects more than "just the facts, ma'am." The details must add up to something that affects and involves readers, making them think or feel— or both.

> *After:* Infantry combat is lonely. In the movies, soldiers huddle together where the camera can see them interacting. In combat, the soldier is alone in the foxhole, dug far enough apart that one shell hits only one foxhole. Each soldier's first enemy is loneliness.

PROBLEM: NO CONNECTION

The draft is neither placed in a larger context—political, historic, sociological, psychological, scientific—nor does it connect with the experience of the reader.

> *Before:* Poverty is terrible. Bad housing crowded together. People sitting an afternoon away on doorsteps or staring out the window. Kids playing without toys. Hopelessness.

SOLUTION

References can be woven within a draft to connect with the reader's experience, using business examples and references for a readership of businesspeople, sports references if the readers follow sports.

> *After:* Studies by Murray (1989) and Morison (1991) have demonstrated that television has brought the poor into intimate contact with the affluent, so the "have-nots" are forced to see how much the "haves" possess—or are invited to purchase— many times in each hour. Starobin (1992) has confirmed what Nestelberger (1980) theorized: the poorer the home, the more hours the television is likely to be turned on.

....

REWRITE WITHIN THE DRAFT

When writers revise their drafts they are tempted to look beyond the page to identify problems and solutions. They try to remember what their teachers or editors have said about this form of writing, they study their notes and look into writing texts, and they consult with friends, family, classmates. But once the writer is within the draft, the most important place to look is within the draft itself. If you read the draft as a stranger, reading what is and what is *not* on the page, the draft will often tell you what it needs.

Here are some examples of student writers engaging in a dialogue with their drafts:

> High school was, to me, even more boring than home. I'm only in college because of the job I had. That really changed me.

> **How was school and home boring? What job? What change?**

> Memo to Manager SuperDooper Supermarkets: Kids could man busy checkout counters. In the Liston Avenue market the checkout lines build up in the later afternoon. I used to work at Bell Road. But it is SooperDooper policy to have high school kids fill shelves when they come on in the afternoon. Older workers could fill shelves.

> **Straighten out the chronology. How about going through a day?**

> Paper route, 1:26 AM papers, used fifth-hand Pontiac I bought from Uncle Jim who was in the Coast Guard, married to my mother's younger sister, she was band director, went to that before school, played tuba cause I was the small guy, I suppose, tuba with feet they said, big noise, played jazz tuba, too, don't laugh, and then school where I had math first period, teacher had a rug, no rugs, he was redhead-blond-prematurely gray, it depended, his wife was the shop teacher, had six fingers—on both hands—no, two on one, four on the other, and . . .

> **Whoa. Slow down. What do these specifics mean? Where are you taking me?**

Development during revision is often a matter of working through the draft, paragraph by paragraph, line by line, sanding, fitting, rebuilding, shaping, caulking, adding, cutting according to the demands of the line.

Boring? No. Because as you develop the draft it grows and changes, teaching you what you don't expect about your subject.

....

EMPHASIZE THE SIGNIFICANT

In developing a draft, make sure you give the proper emphasis to the information you are adding so your meaning will be made clear. In accumulating an abundance of information there is a danger that the draft will be piled up with so many lists and heaps of information that the reader will not be able to see its significance.

Emphasis, of course, is provided by the dramatic nature of certain pieces of information, by the vigor of the writing, but, most of all, by the placement of the information. Where you place the most important information in the sentence, the paragraph, the section, the article, the book is important.

This can be seen most easily in the map of a paragraph:

2nd Point of Emphasis
[important information that will attract a reader]

3rd Point of Emphasis
[attribution and other pieces of less interesting information that needs to be included]

1st Point of Emphasis
[most important information. Will stay in reader's mind and make reader want to continue to read.]

Often the most important information is buried in a paragraph, and the reader zooms right over it. When you have information you must emphasize, the reader remembers best what is at the end of a paragraph, next best what is at the beginning, and least what is in the middle of the paragraph.

This 2-3-1 principle works in key sentences and in larger blocks of writing, but it should not be followed all the time or each sentence, paragraph, and piece will sound the same: ta-boom, ta-boom, ta-boom.

In revision, I consider the 2-3-1 question when I read significant pieces of writing that must be clear to the reader and are totally confusing. Often the important material is buried in the middle and moving it out to the edges will clarify the writing.

Make a photocopy of a page or two of your or someone else's writing, and then cut the paragraphs up, separating the material in the beginning, middle, and end of the paragraph. Then move them around to see how you can deemphasize and emphasize the information being delivered to the reader.

Remember, there may be good reasons to put the key information in the middle of the paragraph or at the beginning. Do not follow this advice slavishly, but consider it if test readers are confused.

··

PACE AND PROPORTION

Two important elements in writing often ignored by writing textbooks are pace and proportion.

Pace is the speed at which the writer causes the reader to move through the text. One way to speed up the pace is to use short sentences and sentence fragments, what one person calls "the English minor sentence": *"Now is the time to vote. Not in the next election. Not tonight on the way home from work. Not during lunch. Right now. On your way to work. This day. This hour. Right now."* The pace can be slowed down by longer words and longer sentences with clotting clauses: *"It is understandable that citizens with multiple responsibilities procrastinate and wait to vote at a later time period that never comes. There is always a meeting, an overdue assignment, a deadline project, a crisis, real or imagined, that delays the electorate until the vote that affects their lives, and the lives of their families, cannot be counted because the polls have closed."*

Proportion is the relationship of the parts to each. Description may need to be balanced by dialogue, facts with people, theories with evidence.

Here is a case where the description overwhelms the dialogue:

> "As town manager, why do you think the town should set aside its zoning regulations to allow a fish processing plant a hundred yards off Main Street?"
>
> The town manager, a neat man with a precise manner, adjusted his rimless glasses, swept his left hand through the head of hair he used to have, tapped his pencil on the hearing table, then opened his old fashioned leather dispatch case. Outside the hearing room, a siren grew loud then faded as it screamed past and in the hearing room those who were for and against the fish plant, neighbors in arms against each other, grew impatient. He found his folder, snapped the base shut, ran his pencil down the right side of the paper then stopped. He looked up and said, "Sixty-five jobs."

And in this case the dialogue overwhelms the description:

> "As town manager, why do you think the town should set aside its zoning regulations to allow a fish processing plant a hundred yards off Main Street?"
>
> The town manager looked up and said, "Sixty-five jobs."

Neither is right or wrong. It depends on what you have to say. The first might be a profile of the town manager, the second a simple report of the hearing.

As you develop your draft, you will confront two key questions: How fast is fast enough? How much is enough?

The issues of pace, the speed with which the reader moves through the draft, and proportion, the length of each section of the draft in relation to the other sections, have to be solved together. When you speed up or slow down a draft, you alter the length of each section, and when you decrease or increase the length of a section, you speed up or slow down the reader's pace.

Proportion is a matter of length, but what is enough exposition or description is affected by the length of other parts. A detailed description of a manufacturing process might allow a detailed analysis; a quick anecdote about the designer of the process might limit a quotation to a sentence. How much ketchup depends, in part, on the size of the burger.

The writer wants to give the reader all the information the reader needs and no more. If there is too little, the reader will stop reading, and if there is too much, the reader will stop reading.

Pace is influenced not only by length but by the way the piece is written. Long sentences and paragraphs slow readers down, short ones speed them up; dialogue increases velocity, description slows it down; verbs and nouns accelerate, adverbs and adjectives apply the brakes.

There is no right pace. It depends on many factors, such as how familiar the readers are with the subject, how specialized their knowledge, how much the writer wants to entertain or inform, appeal to the brain or the heart.

REVISING ACADEMIC WRITING

In developing academic prose the writer must give the reader persuasive evidence that is documented. Academic prose appeals to the intellect more than the emotions, which does not mean it is dull, distant, generalized, boring. All writing in every genre, including academic writing, can achieve the highest goals of fine prose.

The territory of academic writing is the battlefield of ideas. Academics are doing nothing less than battling for control of their readers' minds. In academic writing you see the swordplay between opposing beliefs, theories, concepts. Idea attacks idea as critical minds, disciplined by print, parry and thrust.

To do this, language must be precise and accurate, and to hold the interest of the reader it must be entertaining, lively, sparked by wit. Grace is as important in academic writing as in any other form of composition.

Academic readers, of course, demand substantial, accurate information attributed to reliable sources. They want to know what supports the writer's opinion and where it comes from.

Some inexperienced academic writers think it is possible to build academic writing out of lofty generalizations founded on invisible assumptions. It is not. Academic writing must be specific. It is not enough to list information, however. The specifics must be put in context.

Academic writing is thought laid bare. The writer has to analyze the information, then build a meaning from it. Academic writing is critical thinking written down. It establishes ideas, opinions, theories, propositions, arguments, and it attempts to persuade by a combination of evidence and thought based on that evidence. The writer has to make sure the draft has specifics but also well-founded and developed generalizations that give the specific meaning.

....

NOTES ON WRITING THE PERSONAL ESSAY

The personal essay, if it is successful, looks easy and it should, but the craft that produces easy writing has its own demands. Recently I was asked to speak to a group of professional writers who wanted to publish personal essays, and I wrote the following notes.

- *Respect yourself, your personal vision.* Cultivate an aware self-centeredness of the world around you and the world within you. You have your stories to tell—and a responsibility to tell them. Value what you catch out of the corner of your eye, hear from the next booth or from your own mouth, say when you talk to yourself, think when you are not thinking. Pay close attention to the obvious.

- *The more personal you are, the more universal you will be.* It is the mission of the writer to articulate the inarticulate thoughts and feelings of the reader.

- *The personal must not be private.* The personal must be in a larger context. The essay must have a significance beyond your life, an opinion on the meaning of your experience for you—and your reader.

- *Write with revealing, specific details.* You have seen more than you remember until you write. Use these recovered specifics that resonate for the reader. Specifics make the writing lively, grant you authority, and, unexpectedly, provide universality.

- *Start as near the end as possible.* Don't tell the reader what you are going to do; do it. Weave in background information at the moment the reader needs it.

- *Take your reader on a voyage of discovery.* Write a narrative that reveals what you didn't know you knew. An essay works when I am surprised halfway through with an unexpected meaning I share with the reader.

- *Start with a line, not a subject.* Start with a fragment of language or a haunting image that contains a tension, conflict, contradiction, irony, a problem: write to discover what you have to say.

- *Write with velocity.* Write fast to outrun the censor, force significant accidents of meaning and expression, and create instructive failures.

- *Write out loud.* Writing is read and believed because of voice more than any other element. Write out loud, hearing your draft as it heads toward the page, tuning your natural voice to your content and your reader so each draft has its own consistent voice that will be heard by the reader.

- *Say one thing.* The personal essay must focus on one thing and develop it. Texture comes from the developing material.

- *Less is, indeed, more.* I am surprised at how often 800 words is better than 1,200. Of course, there are times when more is needed, much more. But cutting usually makes a piece of writing stronger. Cut anything that does not move the draft toward meaning. This does not mean writing only in simplistic declarative sentences, but every pause, every detail, every change of tone must move the reader forward.

- *Don't compress, select.* Brevity is not produced by a garbage compactor; select the anecdote, idea, scene, opinion that is central; develop and document it fully.

- *Don't tell, reveal.* Do not insult readers by telling them what they should feel or think. Give them the specific material by which they will create their own text out of their own needs and their own autobiography—and find in it their own meaning.

- *Acceptance is as irrational as rejection.* You are in a personal, irrational business. Do your work. You will learn little from acceptance, less from rejection.
- *Cultivate a good editor.* The good editor helps you write more like yourself. Tell the editor what you need; thank the editor if you get it.
- *Be careful whom you allow to read your drafts.* Most readers—and editors—have expectations of what you *should* say and how you *should* say it: who you *should* be. Seek readers who help you write like yourself and make you want to get back to your writing desk when you leave them.

A PROFESSIONAL CASE HISTORY

You can see if I followed my own counsel as I walk you through a personal essay. This essay/column began when Christopher Scanlan, a close friend and a writer in the Knight-Ridder Washington bureau, wrote a powerful story about the fact that handguns kill 5,000 children under the age of 19 and another 30,000 to 50,000 children are wounded each year. Reading his story, I found myself traveling back to the day my first handgun was placed in my hand.

I start with a line—a fragment of language that itches, has tension, a contradiction, a problem—or an image. This time it was the weight of that 45-caliber pistol that still seemed so natural in my hands. That naturalness and the devastating anecdotes and statistics in the article created a tension in my mind I had to explore in writing.

As I said near the beginning of this chapter, respect your own vision. I am well aware of the fact that there are people who know more about guns than I do, who have used guns more than I have, who have suffered much more combat than I did, but I still have my individual story: the story of a single human being, and each human being's story is worth telling—and hearing. My doubts are similar to the beginning writer's doubts—What do I have to say? Why should anyone listen to me?—and I have to overcome them each day.

I wrote the column—1,278 words—in about 45 minutes. I read and edited it twice, submitted it to Minnie Mae, my wife and first reader, then sent it off to Evelynne Kramer, a superb editor who has helped me write as Don Murray. Many editors try to make you write like someone else, but Evelynne wants me to write like Don Murray.

She called with two concerns: first, a general one that I am writing about World War II too much, using excessive high drama to make points. She fears readers of my *Over 60* column—60 to 70 percent under 60—will say, "Oh, Don's going back to the war." Also, she thought I could tighten the piece up, wondered if the dialogue works, and suggested I'm repetitive about the "power" of the gun.

Writing can always be improved by cutting. Horton Foote, the playwright, says, "I'm a great eliminator. I love to take things out that aren't essential. I've heard that in one of Chekhov's plays he wrote almost a page-long speech. Then he went back and took out everything except the word 'Yes.' I've done that a lot in my time." To emphasize the significant you often have to cut good material, as you will see in this case history, that pulls the reader away from focusing on what is most important.

When my editor mentioned cutting, I marked the scene at the gas station (reprinted here) as a possible cut. I also did a word search on the computer and was shocked to discover I used "power" 17 times, "powerful" twice!

Then I went to work revising, cutting line by line and eliminating. I cut the gas station scene I had marked. It also contained the dialogue she questioned. This became a matter of proportion. I didn't need this scene. It was interesting autobiography, but it wasn't necessary to my meaning and slowed the pace of the essay down. Here's the scene I cut:

> When I was in high school, hanging out at the Amoco station, leaning up against the wall, bragging about what I had not yet done, bored with school, bored with life, an outsider wanting to

be an insider, some kids drove up, tough kids, kids I feared, despised and envied.

"Hey, Murray, get in."

"Nawh."

"We're gonna ride around."

"So?"

"So come along."

"Nawh."

"Why not?"

"I dunno."

And I don't know why I didn't go with them. I didn't know they had a gun but I certainly wanted their acceptance and just being with them would tell others I was tough. I was saved, I suppose, by the incredible *power* of teenage inertia. They held up a gas station, killed the guy who owned it, allegedly with a forty-five like the one the sergeant laid in my hand.

I get a great deal of satisfaction and no sense of failure in making such a cut. It was a good yarn, reasonably well written. There is no way I could tell it was not necessary without writing it and reading it in relation to everything else in the essay.

I also delight in the craft of my line-by-line editing. As I cut, the essay becomes smoother, easier to read, and more powerful: I release it from rhetoric. Here's an example of line-by-line editing:

I was 18 years old and I ~~had power in my hand. Raw power. Primitive power. Magical power, the power of the comics, the power of legends,~~ the power King Arthur's Knights of the Round Table felt in their swords, ~~the power~~ Robin Hood's Sherwood Forest archers felt in their long bows, ~~the power~~ Buck Rogers felt in his space zapper, ~~that~~ Tom Mix felt in his six-gun. ~~I had been initiated into the manly blood rite of guns. And~~ this heavy handgun felt amazingly light in my hand.

Sometimes you have to write badly to write well, and I certainly wrote badly here. In the published column, that passage reads as follows:

I was 18 years old and in my hand I held the power of the sword, the long bow, the six-gun. And it was light in my hand.

Much, much better.

That rough cut brought the draft down to 919 words from 1,278. I felt it was still a bit long. I changed some things in cleaning up the editing and read it again, cutting it down to 882 words. Then another read. Up two words to 884. I sent it in: 1,294 words − 884 = 410 cut from 1,294, 31 percent.

Evelynne Kramer liked it, and here is my personal essay as it ran.

It is 50 years ago this spring that my fingers first curled around a handgun.

The army sergeant had me hold out my right hand, palm up, then he ceremonially laid a 45-caliber automatic pistol on my hand and smiled as my fingers naturally curled around it.

> *"Naturally" is the key word. I give you the dominant impression of the gun and then reveal my hand's reaction to this weapon. I simply wanted to recreate the image, to get out of the way of the writing. And then I go on to establish my authority to write on this subject by providing the reader with specific evidence that I know what I am talking about.*

In my army service I was trained—marksman or better—on three kinds of rifles, two carbines, three submachine guns, light and heavy machine guns, an old fashioned "six-gun" revolver, even a rifled shotgun, but nothing felt as good, as natural, as that forty-five.

> *Notice how I instinctively followed the 2-3-1 paragraph design to emphasize the forty-five. I also want to increase the context and place it within the fantasy world of the young boy or girl.*

I was 18 years old and in my hand I held the power of the sword, the long bow, the six-gun. And it was light in my hand.

> *The line that started me writing the essay might have been "light in my hand." It contains a tension between the "heavy" possibility of the weapon and the lightness or ease with which I wield it.*

With a little training I hit the target in or near the heart every time. We did not shoot to injure, we shot to kill.

"Don't draw your gun unless you intend to use it. Don't use it unless you shoot to kill."

Answer reader's questions when they are asked. Reader asks: "Did you?"

One of my assignments was as an M.P., a military policeman. And more important than the armband, all the paraphernalia we strapped on, the legal nightstick, the illegal slapstick, was my forty-five.

The writer can work in exposition within narrative—how it felt—and how it must feel to kids in the street.

On patrol, my fingers kept straying to my holster, to the butt of my gun; I felt its pressure against my hip like a caress. I was not a kid, I was a man, somebody to reckon with, someone in control, someone mean and tough and hard.

But would I have the courage to use it?

Write long, then short. Short for emphasis.

It was easy.

A fellow paratrooper, drunker than a coot, broke a bottle on a bartender's head in a Tennessee roadhouse and ran out, across a plowed field.

I develop the anecdote I use with abundant detail even if the essay is short. We write short by selecting carefully, then developing what we leave in. If I had left in the gas station anecdote, I would have had less room to develop this anecdote.

I took after him. It was easy to pull out my forty-five, easy to aim and shoot at him running across the uneven ground. Stupid. I missed.

I weave in my basic training instructions. This is pure narrative. Puts the reader within the "I." And note how I follow the natural order I discussed earlier in the chapter. In this case it is a chronological order, a chase, something the reader is familiar with.

"Don't draw your gun unless you intend to use it. Don't use it unless you shoot to kill."

Stop. Kneel. See him against the sky. Aim. Fire. Another miss. But close. He stopped.

He had murdered the bartender, but I didn't know that when I fired. I swaggered in with my terrified drunk and felt great. I was a man for sure.

Note the visual quality of the verb "swaggered."

I used most of the other weapons in combat and along the way got hold of an army forty-five illegally, even had a shoulder holster made for me.

I echo back to the third paragraph, hoping the seed I planted in the reader's mind has survived.

On the troopship home my forty-five and I earned good money as a bodyguard to a kid from New York who ran a crap game. Don't laugh. I heard of at least one combat "hero" tossed overboard on our trip home.

Implies not just combat but a social problem. This writing of the draft was instinctive but now, during the editing, what I have done on instinct has to be considered rationally: What works? What needs work? What doesn't work?

I never used a forty-five to shoot at another human being after that night in Tennessee, but I loved to carry my secret weapon.

Now the lecture. Have I earned the right to do it? A more important question: Will I be more effective if I do not lecture?

Let's witness to true feelings. With my handgun I had nothing less than the power to kill. Mess with me and I can blow you away.

Turn up the heat on the handgun-owning reader.

And—surprise—you don't know I'm carrying. A handgun is usually a hidden weapon, in the belt, in the pocket, in the purse, in the bedside drawer, in the glove compartment.

Turn it up some more.

And it is loaded. No sense in having a gun locked in one room, the bullets in another. What if an intruder . . .

Now connect the handgun-owning reader with the kid on the street.

I am not shocked or surprised kids are carrying—and that many of their parents have their own handguns in bedside drawer or glove compartment. I was intimate with the seduction of the gun and I have to live with my love of that power that lay so easily—so naturally—in my hand.

Weave back to "naturally" and focus on me so reader is not forced into a corner, into a defensive position. We are human beings and that is the problem.

I turned my forty-five in when I was discharged, to the surprise of the sergeant, who probably never reported it and took it home. I don't know why I left it behind, and at times I regretted it. Not now, but in the first years after the war when I was young.

Explicit statement of position. Does it weaken piece?

I am for federal handgun control, for making it illegal for everyone except the police or the military to own or carry a handgun, illegal to manufacture handguns and sell them to anyone but the police or the armed services.

Our nation suffers nothing less than a civil war in our streets, in our schools, in our homes, a war fought with handguns. We should buy back, search out, and confiscate every single privately owned handgun.

If you own a handgun you share—privately, secretly—my seduction by the gun.

Nothing less than mind invasion.

Everyone has their own fantasy: the late-night intruder invading my home, the gang member daring to walk my turf, the holdup man in my store, the man who took "my" woman, the driver cutting me off on the lonely highway, the rapist. No matter the reason, justified by the court or unjustified, the target of every fantasy is the same: another human being.

"Don't draw your gun unless you intend to use it. Don't use it unless you shoot to kill."

INTERVIEW WITH A STUDENT WRITER: KAREN R. EMMERICH

Karen Emmerich was interviewed at the beginning of her freshman year at Princeton when she was facing the pressures of college writing with only what she had learned in high school. She did graduate half a year early and spent the spring studying in the Ithaka Program in Cultural Studies in Greece in Crete. She was awarded second place in a contest established by the Princeton Poetry Center when she was a high school junior, and her poems are being published by Hanging Loose Press. Karen Emmerich was awarded a National Endowment for the Humanities Young Scholar Award and completed a study of William Carlos Williams. She also played the cello in the New York All-State Chamber Orchestra and was a Merit Scholarship finalist at Ward Melville High School in East Satuakat, Long Island, New York. At Princeton, Karen Emmerich works on the *Quarterly Review of Literature*.

What techniques do you use to make sure you have the information to develop a draft? Do you outline and include development in your planning process?

I have always found it nearly impossible to be perfectly prepared—as far as the formulation and logical stringing together of ideas is concerned—before sitting down to begin a draft. Indeed, it would be almost contrary to the purpose of writing to begin with such a foolproof plan of attack. Writing is not merely explanatory, but exploratory, and if one knows beforehand exactly what one is to write, then there is really little reason to begin. On the other hand, some level of preparation is necessary. A familiarity with the topic, with the information, a certain focus of thought, and a specificity of subject are needed to give direction and momentum to the writing. Outlines can be useful in providing this direction—as long as they are not too strictly adhered to, at the expense of the development of the new themes which invariably crop up once the actual writing has begun.

What different techniques do you use to develop a draft when responding to an academic assignment and when initiating your own writing?

Whether I am writing for an assignment or for my own pleasure, I always begin with a freewrite. I sit down, either at my computer or in a comfortable place with a pen and paper, and just write—without regard to grammar or punctuation, without stopping to think about what I'm writing, without monitoring the flow of one idea into another—until I run out of steam, which is usually about 10 or 15 minutes later. Most often I begin with a sentence or phrase which I think will help steer my freewrite in a productive direction. If, for example, I have been asked to write a paper examining an aspect of a certain literary work, I might borrow a representative or provocative phrase from the actual text and proceed from there. This sort of rudimentary structure is often helpful in starting a flow of thought. Then, once my ideas are down on paper, I can review what I've written and determine just what I have to say before sitting down to begin an actual draft.

What attitudes do you find helpful as you develop a draft?

When developing a draft, I find it important not to limit myself to a previously formulated agenda. Writing a paper should always be more than a mere fleshing out of an outline. Although outlines can often be useful tools in the organization of information, they also tend to encourage the compartmentalization of ideas under various subheadings, often at the expense of the overall unity of the composition. If I find myself veering in a certain unanticipated direction, I try to give myself space to explore rather than adhering too determinedly to my original agenda.

What specific process—or processes—do you use to develop a draft?

After completing whatever research and note taking I feel is necessary, I usually begin with a freewrite, which gives me access to my own thoughts on the subject at hand. Then, once I sit down to begin my actual draft, I try to keep with me that same openness of expression which is characteristic of the freewrite. In order not to neglect the general flow of words and ideas, I tend first to spill all of my thoughts out onto the page and then go back to fix up the rough spots, rather than continually worrying over points of grammar and word order and elegant turns of phrase. I find that once I've narrowed my field of vision to do so, it is very difficult to step back and resume work on a larger scale.

How do you change your writing process when doing academic papers and other forms of writing?

My writing process is basically the same for all kinds of compositions, perhaps because my writing style does not differ greatly from one genre to another. I have tried to find my own written voice, one that I can use whether working on a major research paper or an informal essay, rather than, for example, artificially elevating my tone or vocabulary for the purposes of academic writing.

What tools do you use to develop a draft?

Apart from freewriting, there are few other tools that I use in developing a draft. One technique I do find helpful in all types of writing is that of reading what I have written out loud to myself—or, preferably, having someone else read it to me. When I hear my words spoken out loud, I am able to detect grammatical mistakes, ambiguities of language, run-on sentences, and problems of transition from one thought to the next, in a way in which I am otherwise unable to do. This is especially true when another person is reading to me, for they are likely to have trouble with spots which I, as the writer, fully understand. Having others read your work is always helpful, because only they will be able to tell you how successful you have been in communicating your ideas.

How do you know when you've completed the process of development?

I don't believe that I've ever really completed the process of developing a draft. This would imply that the composition had been perfected, that there was no room for improvement. Now, anyone who has ever looked back, after a few years, on a composition they had once considered finished, will realize that a piece of writing is never finished, only set aside or abandoned outright. But it never hurts to work toward that goal of completion: revising and revising and revising as much as you can, and for as long as you can stand it.

What have you learned from playing the cello that you apply to writing?

As a cellist, I feel that there are strong parallels between learning a piece of music and writing a composition. Musicians must be able to master the small details of a piece, without losing sight of the overall style and flow. They must be dedicated to their task, investing a great deal of time, returning to the piece whenever possible to smooth out wrinkles in their work. But there is more to being a musician than just practicing. In order to play well, a musician, I believe, should also listen well. Listening to the performances of others helps to develop a musician's ear, and can give her a sense of what it is possible to do with her own instrument. Similarly, a good writer must first be a good reader. I think that reading the works of other writers has given me an ear for language while also exposing me to the different kinds of things words can be made to do.

What are the most important three things you've learned that other college writers might find helpful?

I think that the ability to freewrite is one of the most useful tools to writers of any level. Not only does freewriting give me access to my own thoughts, but getting into the habit of letting words flow unchecked has, I believe, given me the confidence to use the vocabulary I am most comfortable with when writing academic papers, rather than formalizing my tone to suit the anticipated audience.

Secondly, I have found that one of the hardest aspects of writing a paper is the organization of thoughts into a logical sequence. In order to minimize that difficulty, I tend to set aside temporarily any problems I might be having with the actual structure of the paper until most everything I want to say is down on paper. Then, I read over the entire draft, mentally simplifying each paragraph or section to a general phrase, a "topic sentence," and try to fit these together in a logical order. Afterward, I go back to the computer and shift their respective paragraphs around, adjusting the transitional sentences to suit the new sequence. I might repeat this process several times until I finally reach a sequence I feel comfortable with.

Along the same lines, I often find that the hardest paragraphs for me to write are generally the first and the last—so I tend to start in the middle. Then, once everything is down on paper, and I have adjusted the order of ideas to my satisfaction, I look back over the beginning to see if an introductory paragraph or two is necessary, and read the end to see if anything in the way of a conclusion is still needed. This method enables me to bypass the writer's block associated with that first glaringly blank page, and it also steers me away from writing the usually superfluous introductions and conclusions common in student compositions.

COMMENTARY

I have found it helpful to list my own writing and rewriting procedures for different writing tasks. I have a checklist I can refer to when I return to a similar task, and by writing it down I often see what I am not doing that I should do, what I am doing that I may not need to do, what I might try that I haven't done before. You can extend this as we have in the book by interviewing writers on campus or in town as well as writers in the classroom who may introduce you to new tricks of the writer's trade. I have interviewed my students over the years and they have taught me when they thought I was teaching them.

REWRITE WITH VOICE

Now the fun begins. Now I can play the music of language that will wrap around the words and give them that extra aura of meaning which is the mark of effective writing. It is the music of the language that draws the writer to the writing desk and informs the writer of the meanings and feelings that lie within the subject; it is the music of language that attracts and holds the reader and causes the reader to trust and believe the writer; it is the music of language that provides emphasis and clarity; it is the music of language that makes the writer and the reader *hear* the printed word.

Now, at this crucial moment in the revision process, I have discovered meaning; I have selected convincing evidence; I have read my readers and discovered their needs; I have chosen an appropriate form and constructed an order within it; now I am ready to hear and tune my writing voice.

WHAT DO WE MEAN BY VOICE?

Voice is the magical heard quality in writing. Voice is what allows the reader's eyes to move over silent print and hear the writer speaking. Voice is the quality in writing, more than any other, that makes the reader read on, that makes the reader interested in what is being said and makes the reader trust the person who is saying it. We return to the columns, articles, poems, books we like because of the writer's individual voice. Voice is the music in language.

Many of the qualities writers call *voice* have been called *style* in the past, but writers today generally reject that term. *Style* implies something can be bought off the rack, something that can be easily imitated. *Tone* is another word used, but it seems limited to one aspect of writing. *Voice* is a more human term, and one with which we are familiar.

We all know—and make use of—the individual quality of voice. We recognize the voice of each member of our family from another room; we recognize the voices of our friends down the dormitory corridor or across the dining hall. And we know that voice isn't just the sound of the voice, it is the way each person says things. We enjoy Anne's stories; Kevin's quick rejoinders; the fascinating details Andrea calls attention to; Mark's quiet, straight-faced humor; Tori's mock anger.

Their voices reflect the way they see the world, how they think, how they feel, how they make us pay attention to the world they see. And we are used to using our own voices, plural intended, to tell others our concerns, our demands, our needs.

When we write we should write out loud, hearing what we say as—or just before—we say it. The magic of writing is that the words on the page are heard by the reader. Individual writer speaks to individual reader. The heard quality of speech is put into writing by the writer.

Voice also has a political element. Voice speaks out; voice demands to be heard. The person who has voice is empowered. A person whose voice can be heard in writing has an opportunity to influence the policies of a government, a school, an agency, a corporation, a society. Voices that demand listening may attract hearers who may add their voices to the cause. Information is power, and voice gives focus and significance to information.

DIAGNOSIS: NO VOICE

Lack of voice is the most common reason we stop reading, but we do not name it. Readers don't say, "We abhor the lack of voice here" and put down the article or book. They simply stop reading. Their minds float off the page. They realize they are not reading and turn to something else. They have heard no music where they do not realize there should be music. In the same way, readers who read on do not say, "We are being carried forward on the music of the writer's voice." They just read on, hearing and not knowing they are hearing a voice rising from the page.

As writers, however, we must become aware of the voice of what we write or aware of the lack of a voice. The signs of a draft without voice include the following:

- *No individual human being behind the page.* The page could have been written by anyone. The author is anonymous. The draft was not created by a living human animal but by a machine.

- *No intellectual challenge.* The page does not make intimate combat with the reader's mind. It does not stimulate, challenge, inform, surprise the writer, inspiring the mind-to-mind combat that marks good writing.

- *No emotional challenge.* The page does not engage the reader's emotions, forcing the reader to feel as well as think.

- *No flow.* The reader is not carried forward by the energy of the voice that connects all the elements of writing into a powerful river of language which makes it hard for the reader to escape the page.

- *No magic.* In good writing, the sentence, the paragraph, the page, the entire draft is more than the orderly progression of correctly spelled words marching along in correct grammatical order. Good writing gives the words more meaning than they have while lying separate from each other in the dictionary. The magic of writing is that the voice rises from the spaces between the words as much as from the words themselves carrying meaning to the reader.

Writers write with their ears, listening to the music rising from the page or from the computer screen as they write and rewrite.

....

HEARING THE WRITER'S VOICE

Once you are aware of the importance of voice, read good and bad writers to *hear* the music of their writing—and the marvelous diversity of human voices writing in every genre, for every purpose. Here are some examples of voice I admire and the reasons I admire them.

Here is an account of a few years in the life of Quoyle, born in Brooklyn and raised in a shuffle of dreary upstate towns.

Hive-spangled, gut roaring with gas and cramp, he survived childhood; at the state university, hand clapped over his chin, he camouflaged torment with smiles and silence. Stumbled through his twenties and into his thirties learning to separate his feelings from his life, counting on nothing. He ate prodigiously, liked a ham knuckle, buttered spuds.

His jobs: distributor of vending machine candy, all-night clerk in a convenience store, a third-rate newspaper man. At thirty-six, bereft, brimming with grief and thwarted love, Quoyle steered away to Newfoundland, the rock that had generated his ancestors, a place he had never been nor thought to go.

E. Annie Proulx
The Shipping News

The Shipping News had been recommended to me and when I saw it in a bookstore I picked it up and read these first three paragraphs. I closed the book and bought it. This one I must read. What caught me was the writer's voice. It was individual, powerful, eccentric (another word for individual?) and entertaining. I wanted to hear this voice spin me a story.

In many U.S. school systems, there is a curriculum director whose job it is to puzzle out what a curriculum is. The etymology of the word is promising: it comes from the Latin word *currere*, "to run," and is closely related to the word *curricle*, a two-horse chariot used for short races. Presumably, curricles went around in circles just as curricula trends do in this country, the only difference being that curricle drivers knew they were always going over the same ground, and we often don't. The curriculum director, and those who specialize in this murky science in colleges of education, generally tries to keep the chariots moving in the same direction at roughly the same pace.

Yet the very order suggested by the word "curriculum"—that fixed track upon which the race occurs—seems antithetical to schooling that acknowledges the individual interests and abilities of students. Too often, decisions about what students do at what age are purely arbitrary, and claims by publishers that their work is developmentally sound are only promotional hype. The organization of instruction often shades into regimentation, an interminable forced march through exercises and work sheets. Any misstep, the teacher's manuals imply, might lead to serious problems—like those of the ducklings who didn't learn how to follow their mother at the right time and ended up following the zoo keeper instead.

Thomas Newkirk
More Than Stories—The Range of Children's Writing

Here is a fine example of academic writing in which the author's scholarship is worn lightly and the ideas are presented with clarity, vigor, and grace. This is a seminal study on children's writing, yet there is a place for humor, and you sense the personality of the author from the voice you hear on the page.

There is a loneliness that can be rocked. Arms crossed, knees drawn up; holding, holding on, this motion, unlike a ship's, smooths and contains the rocker. It's an inside kind—wrapped tight like skin. Then there is a loneliness that roams. No rocking can hold it down. It is alive, on its own. A dry and spreading thing that makes the sound of one's own feet going seem to come from a far-off place.

Everybody knew what she was called, but nobody anywhere knew her name. Disremembered and unaccounted for, she cannot be lost because no one is looking for her, and even if they were, how can they call her if they don't know her name? Although she has claim, she is not claimed. In the place where long grass opens, the girl who waited to be loved and cry shame erupts to her separate parts, to make it easy for the chewing laughter to swallow her all away.

Toni Morrison
Beloved

These are two paragraphs from the last chapter of Nobel laureate Morrison's Pulitzer Prize–winning novel. She has the ability to go to the edge of where most of us write and pass beyond it. Her voice has its own fullness, its own passion, its own richness. It is individual. It is her.

To print a document in WordPerfect, you must have selected a printer and specified the port you were using. This was probably done when your copy of WordPerfect was installed. If this is the case, you are ready to print.

You may, however, want to view your current printer selection or change it prior to printing. Or, you may want to use some of the options that are available in the Print dialog box before you send your document to the printer.

WordPerfect Version 6.0
WordPerfect Corporation, Orem, Utah, 1993

That is a good example of a distant, corporate voice. When I shifted to WordPerfect 6.0 I needed other voices to help me.

After entering what you feel is the best piece of written work since Tolstoy, you decide that you want to print it. After all, dragging the computer around and showing everyone what your prose looks like on the screen just isn't practical.

To print a document in WordPerfect—the document you see on the screen (all of it)—do the following:

1. Make sure that the printer is on and ready to print.
2. Press Shift-F7.

You then see the Print dialog box, a busy place where printing and related activities happen. Don't bother with the details. Just blur your eyes at it and keep reading here.

Dan Gookin
WordPerfect 6 for Dummies

This is a fine example of an informal, almost too cute, too friendly writing style, but it was what I needed to get going in this new, complex software program. Note that these two texts are on the same subject, and so is the one that follows.

WordPerfect offers several ways to print your document. You can print directly from the screen all or part of the document that currently appears, or you can print all or part of a document you previously stored to disk. From the screen, you can print the entire document, a single page, a range of pages, or a marked block of text.

Assumptions
- A printer is selected in the Select Printer dialog box.
- The cursor is at the location where you want to print.

Exceptions
- If the page you selected does not appear near the beginning of the document, the printer may pause. WordPerfect scans the pages for the last format settings for margins, tabs, and so on.

Trudi Reisner
WordPerfect 6 Solutions

I needed Dan Gookin's voice to lead me into WordPerfect 6.0, but now I needed a book that was far more detailed and had a voice that was friendly but authoritative, a voice that was halfway between Gookin and the corporate voice of the official manual. I found it after looking at many books in many bookstores. When I read Trudi Reisner I knew that I had found the office companion I needed.

There was a day in my life when I decided to live.

After my childhood, after all that long terrible struggle to simply survive, to escape my stepfather, uncles, speeding Pontiacs, broken glass and rotten floorboards, or that inevitable death by misadventure that claimed so many of my cousins; after watching so many around me, I had not imagined that I would ever need to make such a choice. I had imagined the hunger for life in me was insatiable, endless, unshakeable.

I became an escapee—one of the ones others talked about. I became the one who got away, who got glasses from the Lions Club, a job from Lyndon Johnson's War on Poverty , and finally went to college on a scholarship. There I met the people I always read about: girls whose fathers loved them—innocently; boys who drove cars they had not stolen; whole armies of the middle and upper classes I had not truly believed to be real; the children to whom I could not help but compare myself. I matched their innocence, their confidence, their capacity to trust, to love, to be generous against the bitterness, the rage, the pure and terrible hatred that consumed me. Like many others who had gone before me, I began to dream longingly of my own death.

Dorothy Allison
Trash

This is the opening of the introduction to novelist Dorothy Allison's first book of short stories. You can not deny the authority, power, and toughness of this individual voice that writes with such emotion tempered with talent and craft. And notice the specifics that establish her authority.

Having proposed a biochemical explanation for sensitization, Kandel was ready to take on classical conditioning. By 1981, he and his colleagues had finally got Aplysia to demonstrate what they had claimed was a simple form of conditioning, although the interpretation of the experiment is still hotly disputed. In the earlier experiments the electrical shock to the tail was used to sensitize the snail, causing it to respond more strongly to the tapping on its siphon by withdrawing its gill. But as they played around with Aplysia, trying to uncover other reflexes to study, Kandel and his colleagues found that a tail shock alone could also cause the gill to withdraw. In the new experiments they discovered that if they repeatedly followed a touch of the siphon with a shock to the tail, they could get Aplysia to learn that the touch was a predictor for the shock. Here the electric shock was the unconditioned stimulus. Without any training, it caused the Aplysia to reflexively withdraw its gill. A light tap to the siphon was the conditioned stimulus. At first it caused only a slight gill withdrawal. But if the scientists paired the two stimuli, always following the tap by the shock, the snail would learn to vigorously withdraw the gill just at the tapping.

George Johnson
In the Palaces of Memory

Science writing has produced some of the best voices in our language. It is a particularly disciplined form of writing in which precision of diction and sequence of information must be followed while the author defines each term and makes clear the implication of what is being recorded, yet still manages to communicate the aesthetic importance of what is being reported. Johnson maintains an appropriate distance with his voice. I compare this voice to the whispery voice of the TV golf commentator. Johnson allows us to stand beside him, and as we observe the scientists at work he explains what they are doing and what is important about it.

Bao Yanshan's wife was in labour, about to give birth on her bed at home. Big Dog, the son of Baotown's troop leader, ran shouting down to The Lake to find Yanshan. He came sauntering up, hands behind his back, hoe tucked under one arm, thinking what a common occurrence this had become. The seventh belly, no problem, he was thinking—she's just like an old mother hen dropping another egg. To have it come three months early was just that much better; this time of year there was plenty to eat. But whether it was three months or three days, or three hours, it was not worth getting excited about.

Wang Anyi
Baotown

The author's voice comes through translation, and we hear her beginning her book about the remote village to which she was exiled during China's Cultural Revolution. In these few lines her voice takes us into the place far removed from my New Hampshire home, and also takes me into the mind of a person who is my contemporary, yet lives in a different time.

....

HEARING YOUR VOICE

Voice is often seen as a mystery, an element in writing that is sophisticated, difficult for the student to understand. But I have never had a student who did not come to the first class knowing—and using—many voices.

Before going to first grade, children know there are voices they use in playing they may not use in church, ways of speaking that are not appropriate in front of Grandmother, voices that will win permission from one parent and not another, voices that will make peers come over to play or run away home. We all speak before we have language, when we cry from the crib, with many voices, and it is all those voices that may eventually be turned into voices that will arise from our pages as we write.

Ethnic Influences

We are the product of our racial heritage. There is such a thing as Jewish humor or black humor, which may not be black humor. Sorry, that may be an example of Scottish humor. On my first visit to Scotland I looked up a relative and found an old man digging in a garden. "Are you Donald Bell?" I asked. "Guilty as charged," he answered. I had thought that was a family joke in America and found it was Scottish humor that emigrated to America. It was not a family but a typically Scottish retort. My voice—and yours—is a product of your heritage, all those elements that are passed down in your genes.

Regional Influences

Our voices are also the product of the speaking habits of the area where we are brought up. My speech is urban not country, street language not field language. I speak fast and say Cuber for Cuba and Hahvud Squah for Harvard Square; I speak Boston—perhaps the ugliest accent in America—not Boston Brahmin but Boston working class. Our ears pick up the patterns of speech around us and we make them our own.

Family Influences

Each family has its way of speaking and we learn speech by imitation. No wonder, that for the rest of our lives, we hear the ghosts of those family members who are dead or live far away in our spoken and written voices.

Daily Influences

We all swim in a sea of language. We hear language from radio and television, from the people around us, and, by telephone, from those far away. We respond to language. We read e-mail and snail mail, home pages, flyers, brochures, newspapers, magazines, books. We respond *with* language. We send e-mail and snail mail; write papers and exams and memos; notes to others and ourselves.

YOUR LANGUAGE OR MINE?

It is the responsibility of schools to teach the rules educated people follow most of the time when they speak, write, and read, successfully communicating with each other. But it should also be the responsibility of schools to teach the other times when the rules can be broken to achieve clarity. Language should not be taught as an absolute, a matter of clear right and wrong. The history of language is the history of change; the rules evolve.

This inevitably gets mixed up with status and etiquette. The educated person speaks differently than the uneducated one; the person in power uses language differently from the person out of power; the well-mannered person speaks differently from the uncouth, uncultured one.

I am uncomfortable with those ideas, but they have a truth. I do not come from a well-educated family. They did pay a great deal of attention to speaking properly, but my education isolated me from my background and my family. I recognize the need of people to learn the language of those who have power over them, but I also respect the languages and dialects of all the diverse cultures in our society. The grandmother who brought me up spoke Gaelic, but she would not teach a word of it to me. I was to be an American and to speak American. Sadly, I became monolingual and was cheated of the heritage of Gaelic literature, oral and written, with which I should have been familiar.

I am writing a textbook of revision and inevitably I seem to say "Write like me," and that makes me uncomfortable. And yet, the world judges you, more than it should, by how you speak and write. If you want to be heard, to be empowered, you have to find your way to use our language, not your own, and eventually to enrich our language with your own.

THE IMPORTANCE OF YOUR VOICE

Voice is the most important element in writing. It is what attracts, holds, and persuades your readers.

Significance

Voice illuminates information. Voice makes what appears to be insignificant information significant, and an ineffective voice can make what is significant for readers appear to be insignificant.

Character

Voice is a matter of character. The great essayist E.B. White once said, "Style results more from what a person is than from what he knows." When we write we reveal how we think, how we feel, how we care, how we respond to the world.

Trust

An effective voice demonstrates it is an authority on the subject. It speaks with confidence in specific terms. It is sure enough to qualify, to admit problems, to allow weaknesses of argument; it does not shout and bang the desk but speaks quietly to the individual reader, for writing is a private act—one writer to one reader. The writer's voice endeavors to earn the trust of the reader.

Music

Language is music. Writing is heard as it is read. The effective voice is tuned to the message, the situation, and the reader. The music of the writer's voice, similar to the music accompanying the movie, supports and advances the meaning of the entire text.

Communication

The effective voice can be heard, respected, and understood by a reader. Writing is a public act performed in private and received in private. Both reader and writer are alone. The writer must anticipate the language of the reader so that the act of writing will be completed when the writer's message is absorbed by the reader.

THE EXPECTED VOICE

Society has voices it expects from us according to the message we have to deliver and the place it will be delivered. The victorious locker room voice is different from the losing voice; the funeral voice different from the party voice. When we read science fiction, a newspaper sports story, a war report in a magazine, an economics or composition textbook, we have expectations.

The effective writer knows what the reader expects and decides to write within or against those expectations. But if the writer works against the expectations—using a poem to report on a football game, a narrative as a corporation annual report—the reader must be informed in some way that the writer is aware of going against expectations. The reader must be prepared because the expectations of the reader are always strong.

THE FORMAL VOICE

In school and at work, we learn the traditions of the formal voice, the literary research paper, the lab report, the nursing notation, the business memo. These formal traditions are usually rigid for good reason. The doctor scanning the nurse's nighttime notations is not looking for an aesthetic experience or a philosophical essay on pain, but clear, specific information to help modify treatment.

THE INFORMAL VOICE

The informal voice also has its own traditions. When we write a thank you note to Aunt Agatha, a humor column in a college newspaper, a note stuck on a door to tell a friend where we are eating, we also follow traditions. The style may be casual, but it is usually in a casual tradition. Jeans and sneakers may be just as traditional as tux and gown. We need to know the tradition, then try to vary it if the tradition interferes with the delivery of our message.

GENRE VOICES

Narrative, journalism, drama, poetry, biography, and autobiography all have their own traditions that you can discover by asking people in that field to tell you the tradition, where it is published, or by reading in that form. There are many languages of lyric poetry or of jazz, folk, or rock lyrics, but each belongs to a tradition that can be defined and described.

THE VOICE OF THE DRAFT

Traditional education focuses on the traditional voice; untraditional education focuses on the personal voice. I think they both miss the target. We need to know how to use the conventions of traditional language, and we need to be able to hear the sound of our personal voice, but the focus should be on the voice of the individual draft. Voice, as we have said, is a matter of situation; what is appropriate for one message, in one genre, for one reader, may not be in another.

Listen to the Voice of the Draft

We need to train ourselves to listen to the voice that emerges from the draft, we need to hear how language is being used in this particular case. Of course, what we will hear will be a blend of personal and traditional voices woven together for this particular purpose. That should provide the focus: What is needed here? What is strong and right? What needs to be extended and developed?

We have to be able to work at the console of language, mixing the tracks we hear so they work together to produce a combined voice—the voice of the draft—that will communicate our meaning.

Choose a personal experience that has affected your life and take 10 minutes to describe it in writing. If you work on a computer, turn the screen off, if not, try not to pay attention to how your draft looks. Speak the draft out loud, hear what you are saying as you are saying it, follow the beat, the rhythm, the tone, the melody of what you are saying. Stop after 10 minutes and read your draft aloud to hear your voice rise from the page.

....

CASE HISTORY OF A
PROFESSIONAL WRITER

I used to start the day with an informal breakfast club until the members became obsessed with healthy food and exercise. It wasn't that they ate healthy food and exercised—sometimes they did, mostly they didn't—but they talked about it all the time. I passed through anger to guilt—I wasn't eating right or exercising—to boredom to wondering about the real old-timers—I'm only 72—I know who pay no attention to diet or exercise and seem to keep going just fine into their eighties and nineties, even beyond.

A piece like this depends on voice so I test the voice in the lead. It only takes a few lines to hear the music of a draft. I play with leads in my head and then try some on the computer screen:

> I'm fed up with health food. I want to start the day with a plate of well-greased animal parts collected in a sausage that drips with flavor, two real eggs over easy, hash brown potatoes sparkling with droplets of fat, buttered toast and apricot jam. The health food of my childhood.

***

> When I was a skinny child the doctor told my family to fatten me up—mashed potato WITH gravy, bread with butter and jam; meat dripping with blood; thick soups; ice cream ON pie; snacks, seconds, thirds, more and more and more until I grew into the pear-shaped adult of their dreams. Now my friends peck at leaves, phony meat, deflavored eggs, and even drink healthy, un-flavored water. They are skinny—and unhappy. They must be.

***

> I used to go out to breakfast with friends. Now I draw the cur-tains, turn off all the lights but a small one in the kitchen, and eat my bacon, eggs, toast and marmalade, and caffeine coffee,

quickly, furtively, hoping the diet police will not break down the kitchen door.

***

I have 134 cholesterol and yet have had one heart attack, one triple bypass, one angioplasty. Before the heart attack I dieted and took 34 health pills a day—fish oil and stuff I don't want to know where it comes from. So much for health food.

***

When I was a boy everyone was obsessed with bowel movements. Some of my friends even had to keep charts. My mother just made sure. When I had a stomachache, I had a laxative until my appendix blew up and I almost died.

I was 15 and I have been a health cynic ever since. Tell me it's good for me and I doubt it.

***

When a friend of mine got cancer she felt betrayed. She had jogged, eaten organic, meditated. She couldn't get cancer, but she did.

She recovered from her cancer quicker than from her anger. She had made a deal with God and paid attention to diet fashion. She didn't know that God makes no deals.

***

I'm a grown-up. I survived the food fads of my childhood—fat is good—and I will survive the food fads of adulthood—fat is bad. Just don't make every meal a competition to see who can eat better.

I don't care what you eat—garden burgers, raw carrots, kiwi, sprouts without dressing—just don't smear your smug on me.

I finally decided to lighten up when my writer friend Don Graves told me how he pretends he only has a rotary phone when automated messages try to make him choose touch tone alternatives. I began to hear the voice of an old-timer who has made modern times adjust to him rather than the other way around. I listened and wrote the following column, which is an exercise in voice: my column voice and the created voice of Ephraim Graves.

When I get confused about what the news says about how I should live my life, I drive out to the Piscataqua Pond and visit Ephraim Graves. He is 111 years old, cuts his own wood, grows his own vegetables, kills his own protein, and has never been to a doctor in his life.

"Mr. Graves," I ask (he comes from a more formal era, I'd never call him Eph), "I've got dry knees."

"Kinda like sandpaper in the joints in the morning, kinda grindy?"

"Yep. You're right."

"What you have is ungreased joints. Had the same thing when I was young, 'bout 71, maybe 2. Bad case of ungreased joints. I doubled my morning bacon to eight strips, two over easy eggs, started to butter my pie. That made the difference."

"Butter your pie?"

"'Course."

"Pie at breakfast. That'll kill you."

"Ain't yet."

"Maybe because you exercise."

"I don't believe in it."

"But you cut your own wood."

"Who would if I didn't, huh? That's a chore, not exercising. I see them running by here all the time. Gives them the jiggles. Jogging, they call it."

"The jiggles?"

"Running shakes up your organs, jiggles them. Kidneys, liver, intestine, stomach, heart, they're all jammed into the same area, run and they bang into each other. Get bruised. The jiggles, bad stuff."

"I worry about forgetting names."

"I revel in it. Can't remember the names of my first two wives. Good thing, only make me mad. Same as the kids. They tried to put me in a home. Forget them."

"You don't let life get to you, do you? Just maintain a kind of transcendent peace."

"What kinda peace?"

"I mean you don't let things bother you."

"I let everything bother me. Angrifying yourself is good, keeps the blood circling."

"What angrifies you?"

"Mosquitoes. Stray dogs. Neighbors. Grown up people that ride bicycles three abreast down the highway. Love to scatter them. Kids with baseball caps on backwards. Republicans. Democrats. People that wear metal in their nose, tongues, God knows where else. Clothes too large for 'em. Wear advertisements on their shirts. Salad bars. Don't eat raw vegetables. Cook 'em first. Broccoli. Idiots that buy designer water. Canned laughter on TV. Sushi. Taco. Pizza. Bagels. Eat American I say."

"All that makes you mad."

"Right. I get up in the morning calm, peaceful like, then I turn on the TV. The world infuriates me. Dole. Clinton. Princess Di. The Red Sox. I feel the rage start to percolate. Know I'm alive. Angry. Mad."

"Doesn't that well, cause stress?"

"Damn right. Need stress to keep alive. Gets the heart beating, stretches the arteries, magnifies the brain."

"I thought stress kills."

"Naw. Happiness. Content. They kill. First you're bored, then you're dead, you don't even know the difference. Get aggravated, that's the way to live. Look at those of us who have survived. We're crusty, grumpy, growly, cantankerous."

"Proud of it?"

"Damn right. None of them smiling little drawings for us. Smilies, they call 'em. Not for me."

"No 'have a good day'?"

"Never. Who's going to tell me how to live my day? I want a bad day, full of irritation. No more boring days for me. I want some Moxie in my life."

"What is a good, I mean a bad, day for you?"

"I like to start the day by hanging up on some telephone solicitor. 'Don't want whatever you're peddling.' Slam down the receiver. Feels great. Grand way to start the day. Better, the mail comes and I get overcharged on a bill. I love to argue about a bill. Got a trick for you."

"What is it?"

"When them dang machine voices on the phone tell you to punch one if you have a touch tone phone, don't."

"But I have one. Should I lie?"

"It isn't lying when you're talking to an electronic robot. Stay on the line. They'll think you have a rotary phone. A human being comes on the phone. You can be nasty to a human being."

"Nasty?"

"That's what gets your dang blamed computer bill corrected—good old rage—and it's what keeps you young."

"Being nasty?"

"Nothing like it. Elixir of youth. Stay stressgravated and you'll stay around—and have fun. But never admit it."

"Never admit what?"

"Being old. Angry. Nasty. Mean. I love it. Heard a young fella say the other day, 'Watch out, here comes old Graves. He's the nastiest old man I've ever known.' Best day of my life."

"Keeps you young?"

"Who wants to be young? More fun being old—and mean."

The column got an enormous response and most who responded wanted to visit Ephraim. Of course, Ephraim only lives behind the screen on my monitor. I may go there to see him again, but the effectiveness of the column depends on voice—my voice tuned to an individual vision of our world.

I hope you can hear old Ephraim Graves speaking from the page, and I hope you can hear your own voice, tuned to an individual of your own, come aloud on your page.

CHAPTER 8

REWRITE TO EDIT

When I edit, I become the reader's representative. I distance myself from my ego and try to read as a stranger. Years ago the poet John Ciardi said, ". . . the last act of the writing must be to become one's own reader. It is, I suppose, a schizophrenic process. To begin passionately and to end critically, to begin hot and to end cold; and, more important, to try to be passion-hot and critic-cold at the same time."

If you watch a painter at work, you will see her step back from the canvas, look critically at what has been done, then return to do more. It is not a painful process for me to step back. In fact, I find it fun to detach myself from my work and read it as a stranger. I discover what I have done as well as what I have not done—and must do. I am still discovering what I have to say and how I may be able to say it.

Yet many beginning writers find it difficult to stand back and take what they think is a final first draft and treat it like a beginning draft needing change, cutting, adding, moving around. To help you, I have developed a list of ways to distance yourself from a first draft that may seem finished.

TWENTY WAYS TO UNFINAL A DRAFT?

When your draft suffers from premature completion, try one—or two or three—of these activities to make the draft alive again.

1. *Listen to the draft.* Learn to hear what the draft is saying. It may be wiser and more interesting than what you intended to write.

2. *Welcome the unexpected.* What contradicts, challenges, qualifies, questions what you intended to write is evidence of thought and may be worth exploring in a new draft.

3. *Expand what works.* Push the edge. Take what is most successful, strongest, and well written, and develop it further, beyond where you think it can go.

4. *Tune the music of the draft.* Hear what the voice of the draft is saying. What does it emphasize; what makes the voice angry, sad, worried, happy, confident, shy, combative? Follow the voice toward its meaning.

5. *Start closer to the end.* Introductions are not necessary in most drafts. Start as near the end as you can and fold in the information readers need when they need it.

6. *Cut the end.* It is too late to tell the reader what you have said, why you have said it, how important it is for the reader to know it.

7. *Cut or extend the length.* Play with the length. You may just be telling readers, not giving them the evidence they need. Realize that shorter is usually better than longer.

8. *Play with a new focus.* Move back or in close; narrow or expand the focus of the draft.

9. *Reconsider the audience.* Limit, extend, or switch the readers you are trying to reach.

10. *Put the draft in a new context.* Each draft has its own context, the place it fits into the world. It can be illuminating to see the draft make a new connection with the world.

11. *Make new connections.* Meaning is constructed as specific pieces of information connected to other information. Change the connections to discover new meanings.

12. *Reorder the draft.* Write backward, sideways, or start in the middle to see what a new logic reveals.

13. *Change the pace.* Each piece of writing moves at its own pace, slowing down to allow readers to comprehend, speeding up to keep them interested.

14. *Unbalance the proportions.* There is an internal relationship between the size and weight of each part of a draft. Play with a new relationship.

15. *Try a new genre.* The draft may work better in a new genre or it may be improved by crossing genre, using narrative to argue, a profile to tell a story.

16. *Add new evidence.* New documentation or new forms of documentation, anecdote instead of statistic, quotation instead of generality, may produce a better draft.

17. *Look for instructive failure.* The moment of failure as in a scientific experiment may be the moment of revelation. Syntax often breaks down at the point of discovery.

18. *Role-play a reader.* Imagine a specific reader and read through that person's eyes to see what is being said and what may be said.

19. *Use a test reader.* Tell a reader the kind of reading you need—a quick read for meaning or order, a line-by-line read for language—and consider the response.

20. *Observe the draft.* Study how the draft is evolving. The struggle within a draft may be between the form you are imposing and the form its meaning needs.

····················

THE ATTITUDE OF THE EDITING WRITER

I used to hate to rewrite, but my attitude changed with the experience of editing. I learned to be comfortable operating surgically on my draft. I saw how it improved my drafts and began to enjoy it. Here are some attitudes I bring to editing.

WRITING IS EDITING

It is not an admission of failure when you have to edit. It is a normal part of the process of making meaning with language. Editing is not punishment, but opportunity.

IMAGINE THE READER

To get distance on my own copy I often become the reader. I think of a person I know whom I respect but who has no interest in the subject I am writing about. I may walk around my office like that person walks, imitating their gestures, even their speech patterns. Then I read my words through that person's eyes, line by line.

In this way I see my writing from a stranger's point of view. Not someone who is a lunkhead but an intelligent person I want to reach who does not share my assumptions about the subject.

MY EAR IS A BETTER EDITOR THAN MY EYE

We spoke before we wrote, historically and individually. Writing is not quite speech written down, but it is speech transformed so that it may be heard. The voice lies silent within the page, ready to be turned on by a reader. Writing is an oral/aural act, and we do well to edit out loud, hearing the text as we revise and polish it.

THE DRAFT WILL TELL YOU WHAT IT NEEDS

I have learned to respect my draft. Writing is not an ignorant act. Something was happening when the draft was being written. Writers know the contradiction of art: there is usually reason in accident. Try to understand the draft on its own terms. Do not make it what you or the world expects, but what the draft itself commands.

WELCOME SURPRISE

Many people fear surprise. They hunger for control, and so do I in many parts of my life. But I have trained myself to remember that it is the unexpected that instructs me, the accident, the failure. When I say what I do not expect to say, it is evidence I have been thinking. I have to stop and consider the surprise. It may not mean anything this time, but most times it will mean a great deal. It will point me to my meaning.

LANGUAGE IS ALIVE AND CHANGING

This writer sees language as ever changing. I may not like all the changes—I growl at split infinitives and grump when people use *host* as a verb or *fun* as an adjective—but most of the time I delight in our changing language and work as a writer at the edge of tradition. That is where the writer is using language to say what has not quite been said before in a way that has not quite been heard before.

The writer's rule is not to judge what is right or wrong—correct or incorrect—but what works and what doesn't. No decision about language can be made in the abstract any more than a surgeon should decide to operate without first examining the patient. All editing decisions are context oriented; what may be correct in one place may not be in another. Writing's job is not to be correct but to communicate meaning.

ACCEPT LIMITATIONS

I accept the limitations of my craft—the assigned length of the draft, the expected form and tone, the targeted reader, the deadline—then go beyond the acceptance to view the limitations as a creative challenge. The mural is different from the miniature, the song from the opera, the jazz combo from the big band. The limitations of any art contribute to its breakthroughs; it is not discipline or freedom alone that are at the center of craft but the tension between freedom and discipline.

ESTABLISH ACHIEVABLE STANDARDS

Student writers and professional writers, myself certainly included, tend to dream an impossible draft. That is a certain route to failure. We give up before beginning the draft, knowing we can't do it; we quit while drafting because we are not living up to an imaginary standard; we toss the final draft because it doesn't measure up to an unreasonable standard.

INTERVIEW YOUR DRAFT

The draft will tell you what is needed, if you know how to ask. The skillful writer is first a skillful reader who can read what is on the page and what is not on the page rather than what the writer hopes is on the page.

- *What is the one thing I wanted to say, the single, most important message I intended to deliver?*

  Writing is thinking, and the best writing usually produces a draft that surprises us. It says what we did not expect. The writer should not feel a sense of failure but satisfaction when this happens. Then the writer has to decide whether to force the writing back to its intention as the writing assignment may demand or follow the draft toward its evolving meaning.

- *What single message does the draft deliver?*

  It may help to underline that message if it is established in a single, clear sentence within the draft or write it out in a sentence so it will be a North Star during the revision process.

- *To whom is the message being sent?*

  If the message has a specific reader, the writer must know the reader and anticipate that reader's response. If there is no specific reader, the writer should call to mind a specific person who is intelligent but does not know the subject or care about it. Then the writer should read the draft from that person's point of view. Of course, the writer is always the first reader, and effective writers learn to distance themselves from a draft and read it as a stranger would.

- *What form or genre will deliver the information the reader needs most effectively?*

  The most effective forms grow organically from what needs to be said. We have discussed how rhetorical forms result from the study of what has worked for writers in the past. The writer who is trying to discover meaning in material and communicate it has to look at the writing task, the material, and the prospective reader to see what form will deliver that meaning to that reader.

The material shapes the form. It may be problem/solution, a narrative, an argument, an explanation, a case history, a report. With some writing assignments, a specific form is required and the writer has to adapt the form to the material.

- *Does everything in the draft support or advance that message?*

In effective writing, one meaning dominates and everything supports that meaning, grows from that meaning, develops that meaning.

- *Where are the strongest places or what are the most effective elements in the draft?*

Effective revision is usually more the product of developing and extending the strengths within the draft than correcting errors in the draft.

- *Where are the greatest failures in the draft?*

Failure is instructive. Often the place where the syntax breaks down or the structure takes an illogical turn is the point where the writer is starting to say something important the writer does not yet know how to say. It may be a point of discovery, not failure.

- *Are the reader's questions answered* when *they will be asked?*

It is helpful to write down the questions the reader will ask— not the ones you want them to ask, the ones they *will* ask— and then put them in the order the reader will ask them.

- *Is the draft written with information, not just language?*

Remember that the reader is not hungry for your fancy words, your ability to turn a mean phrase, but for specific, accurate information.

- *Is each point supported by documented evidence?*

Do not depend on the reader taking anything on trust.

- *Is the voice of the draft appropriate to the subject and the reader?*

In revising, the writer must read the draft aloud and tune the music of the draft so it supports the meaning. The voice of the draft is what makes readers read and trust the writer.

- *Does the draft exist within the shared world of the writer and reader?*
  Everything in the draft should be in context; it should ring true to the experience the writer and reader share.
- *Is there anything that can be cut?*
  E.B. White, the great essayist, quoted his teacher Will Strunk as saying, "Vigorous writing is concise. A sentence should contain no unnecessary words, a paragraph no unnecessary sentences, for the same reason that a drawing should have no unnecessary lines and a machine no unnecessary parts. This requires not that the writer make all his sentences short, or that he avoid all detail and treat his subjects only in outline, but that every word tell." I kept that quotation over my desk for decades until it was etched on the inside of my forehead.
- *Does the typography and visual layout of the draft support and make the message clear?*
  The reader is influenced by the professional appearance of the draft.
- *Are the portions of information adequate?*
  The reader is hungry for information and that hunger must be satisfied.
- *Will the reader keep reading?*
  The pace of the draft should be slow enough so the reader can absorb the information and its meaning, fast enough to keep the reader interested. The proportion between the parts of the draft often determines the pace.
- *Is there anything—spelling, grammar, mechanics—that gets between the reader and the message?*
  George Orwell, the British writer who certainly influenced the way I write my essays, proposed this list in his famous piece "Politics and the English Language":
  i.   Never use a metaphor, simile, or other figure of speech which you are used to seeing in print.
  ii. Never use a long word where a short one will do.
  iii. If it is possible to cut a word out, always cut it out.

iv. Never use the passive where you can use the active.

v. Never use a foreign phrase, a scientific word, or jargon word if you can think of an everyday English equivalent.

vi. Break any of these rules sooner than say anything barbarous.

George Orwell

- *What does a test reader say?*

  Be careful who you have read your draft. My rule is to use someone who makes me want to write when I hear his or her response. That response may be critical, but a good reader motivates me to rush to fix the draft. The writer should also be aware that most readers have expectations and are uncomfortable when the draft does not say what they expect in the way they expect it. It helps to tell the test reader what kind of reading you want: Would you believe this? Would you keep reading? Are there any spelling or punctuation errors you can see? What does the draft say to you? Where do I say too much or too little? What evidence do you need?

- *What do you expect the reader to do after finishing the draft?*

  We write to make the reader think, feel, and act. We should try to predict the response of the reader and revise to achieve the response we want.

- *If you were the reader, would you do it?*

  If you wouldn't feel, think, or act because of reading your draft, the reader won't either.

SOLUTIONS TO COMMON EDITING PROBLEMS

As we edit our drafts, we begin to recognize some problems that occur over and over again. You may want to make a written as well as a mental list of some of those problems and their solutions. Here is mine.

HOW DO I RECOGNIZE SURPRISE?

Effective writing is built on recognizing and developing the strength of an early draft. The strength is usually what surprises the writer, but how does the writer recognize surprise? The surprise is often an instructive failure, but how does the writer see what is an instructive failure and what is true failure?

- I am saying what I have not said before.
- I am saying what I have said before in a new way.
- My voice contradicts my meaning and I listen to the voice.
- I contradict intent.
- The syntax breaks down: I am trying to say what I do not yet know how to say.
- The draft tries to use an unexpected genre.
- The flow of language takes a sudden turn.
- The writing comes easily.
- The voice reinforces the meaning.
- I discover I know what I did not know I knew.
- I am making unexpected and appropriate connections between specific information I did not think had a relationship.
- The specifics resonate.
- I am following the draft as it rushes toward its own meaning.
- The draft asks questions I—and the reader—must have answered.
- I receive novelist and critic Edmund Wilson's "shock of recognition": this is true.
- I try to change the structure or the order within the structure and can't.
- A test reader recognizes a strength I didn't.
- The draft poses a problem that would be interesting to solve.

HOW TO READ TO EDIT

It is wise to do several quick readings of a draft, focusing on one form of exploration at a time, rather than trying to do them simultaneously.

Reading the Whole

The writer needs to step back from the word-by-word, phrase-by-phrase, sentence-by-sentence concentration essential to produce a draft and take an aerial view of the entire draft, not worrying—during this reading—about spelling, mechanics, typography, neatness. I have trained myself to become the detached reader—changing from the possessive, defensive writer of the draft to a stranger who is reading what actually appears on the page—in a matter of minutes, say after a mug of coffee. But if I cannot achieve the distance I need, that is, the reader's view of the draft, I imagine I am someone I know and respect who is not interested in the subject. That gives me the distance I need.

Reading the Parts

After reading the whole, I move a bit closer to see the parts of the whole, the sections that develop each part of the overall meaning. I read to find their relationship: Are they in the order the reader needs to come to the final meaning? Are they paced so the reader will continue to read—fast enough to keep the reader awake and interested, slow enough so that it is not a blur but gives the reader time to absorb the meaning of the draft? Do the proportions of the draft support the meaning—long enough but not too long? What is the relationship between the sections; do they interact in an effective way?

Reading the Line

Once the writer has the vision of the whole draft and sees how the sections fit the vision of the whole, the writer can read the draft closely, line by line. Each word, each phrase, each sentence, each paragraph is scanned to see how it fulfills the vision. The reading writer needs to keep moving in close but never to allow the eye to focus entirely on details. Reading line by line means seeing how the details support and develop the meaning that the entire draft is designed to communicate to a reader. Many people read too closely too early and get lost in the details of writing—word choice, spelling, grammar, punctuation—before they have solved the larger problems of meaning, development, organization, proportion.

Reading Out Loud

And all through this, I hear the voice of the draft. *Voice,* the writer's word for style, is thought of as a final, superficial concern, the living room pickup before a guest's arrival. But voice is not superficial; indeed, it may be the most important element in writing. It is the way, more times than not, that I discover meaning in reading my notes and early drafts. I find that meaning is often revealed through the music of the draft the same way that the meaning of the movie scene is revealed by the musical score. The voice of the draft is tuned to the meaning of what is being written.

HOW TO EDIT A BORING DRAFT SO IT ISN'T

All of us face writing tasks that are boring. We have done it before, and before that: a report for the corporate record that may never be read, yet another term paper, a revision required when it is not necessary, a rejected proposal that is being submitted to yet another agency, a personal report that must follow a specific form, an essay exam at the end of an uninteresting course and, worst of all, another version of a well-written piece of writing that you have done several times before. Once it was frightening and demanding, now it is far too familiar.

I know. Today I face my 445th newspaper column, and this is the third edition of a textbook that I thought was fine each time I finished an edition. And I will start the sixth edition of another textbook after I finish this.

First I have to break down any task longer than a few pages into brief morning tasks. I produce more when I write less at a sitting but return frequently. I work in spurts—15, 20, 30, 45, 60, 90 minutes. More than that and my attention wavers; I become sloppy.

I must decide on specific tasks that can be fitted into an appropriate writing period. And the earlier in the day, the more I can accomplish in a shorter period of time.

I also need to reward myself after I finish a task: one section and a cup of coffee, three pages and a walk around the yard, ten pages and I can read a few pages of a novel, a chapter and I can go to a bookstore. The breaks revive me and I can go back to the next task.

Once I am within the task, here are some of the ways I make boring writing interesting to me—and, I hope, the reader.

I take advantage of anything that will allow me to see the familiar subject in a new way. My closest friend was complaining about starting a book that is published annually. He had done it last year and the year before that. At first it was a challenge, now it is routine. He asked me, "Do you find writing a new edition of one of your books boring?"

I answered, "Yes, I suppose, but. . . . Well, I break the book down into specific daily tasks—what is new, what needs to be cut, what needs sharpening and brightening."

I knew I hadn't answered his question adequately, and I saw that as an opportunity to figure out what to do. If I figured it out in writing, I would have the draft of a section for this edition. It wouldn't be boring to write because I would be learning something I could apply to other writing tasks, and it wouldn't be boring for my readers, since they all face writing tasks that have become too familiar.

The novelist Tom Williams once told me that the writer should have "a technical problem to solve in each draft to keep him interested." This problem should be a secret from the reader, it should never show, but it makes each new story or book—and each revision—fresh for the writer and, therefore, for the reader.

I have followed his wise counsel. The technical problem may be a small one but it challenges my craft as I work on a page, a section, a chapter. Here are some of the technical problems I have set for myself:

- Switching from first person to third or back.
- Retuning the voice of the draft or the narrator.
- Writing in the present tense or the past.
- Using shorter sentences or paragraphs.
- Using longer, more fully developed, sentences and paragraphs.

- Writing in the active voice.
- Cutting to a specific length.
- Expanding to a specific length.
- Appealing to a different audience or an additional audience.
- Changing the documentation from anecdotal to statistical or reversing it, depending on academic citations or personal experience.
- Adding or cutting quotations.
- Using dialogue.
- Switching the genre from prose to poetry to essay to dramatic scene to memo to argument.
- Changing the point of view from which the subject is viewed.

This is all play but play with a purpose. I make the changes to see if they will reveal the subject with greater insight or clarity, if they will hold readers' interest and persuade them.

The subject, the form, the audience may be familiar, but when I consciously establish a technical problem, I become interested in solving the problem. It only takes me a line or two, perhaps a paragraph, when I am within the draft, not only discovering how to say it anew but also usually discovering that I have new things to say.

The changes I am making may seem small at first, but often the result surprises me. As the artist Cézanne said, "I could keep myself busy for months without moving from one spot, just by leaning now to the right, now to the left." A new seeing does not mean a new view but a new way of looking at the familiar.

I rarely see what can be done to make a familiar text new by looking at it from a distance. I have to put my pen or cursor to work, striking out, inserting, moving words, phrases, sentences, paragraphs around, and I find I am lost in the work. As the sculptor Alexander Calder said, "If you keep working, inspiration comes."

In the most apparently boring writing tasks, I discover a joy in craft. The making provides its own pleasure and its own importance. As Don DeLillo says, "Working at sentences and rhythms is probably the most satisfying thing I do as a writer. I think after a while a writer can begin to know himself through his language. He sees someone or something reflected back at him from these constructions." There are few tasks that appear to be as boring as fixing language that you feel doesn't need fixing; there are few tasks as exciting as following language that unexpectedly comes alive under your hand, making the familiar strange word by word, line by line.

And, of course, some things do not need to be changed: what needs to be said is said with clarity and grace. It is just as much an act of craft *not* to change as it is to change. The purpose of writing is not to show the writer at work but to discover meaning and communicate it directly to a reader who should not be aware of the writer but the writing.

THE CRAFT OF EDITING

When I write and rewrite there is an unconscious element in what I do. I do not want to become so aware of how my feet are placed as I go downstairs that I will cross them and tumble down three flights. I often work instinctively. But as I pass through the revision process, the writing becomes self-conscious. I need to be aware of how I do what I do, of my reader, of tradition, of my purpose.

THE TOOLS OF REVISION

Beginning writers have too much respect for their written drafts. They have been taught to respect—or fear, or stand in awe of, or to admire without question—the printed text. The writing, especially if it is typed, appears finished.

The experienced writer likes nothing so much as despoiling a neatly printed text. The writer cuts and adds and moves around and puts back what was just cut and discards and redrafts.

Now I write on a computer where my best friend is the button marked DELETE. I draft and revise while always having a neat, readable text on my screen. But for decades before computers I revised, and my office still has the tools I used—and occasionally still use— to make my final draft look easy, natural, even spontaneous.

My tools are a wastebasket, large; scissors; glue, stapler, cellophane tape; a black, thick-line felt marker; an extrafine black pen. I can discard, cut and paste, cross out and insert.

Here are some of the ways the writer marks an evolving draft:

Cross out	The ~~lazy~~ dog runs slowly.
Take out	The lazy dog runs slowly.
Put back in	The ~~lazy~~ dog runs slowly.
Transpose	The lazy dog slowly runs.
Insert	The lazy dog saunters ~~runs slowly.~~
Move	The lazy dog runs slowly.
Period	The lazy dog runs slowly.
Capital	the lazy dog runs slowly.

Mark the draft so you can see the changes, and read the draft as it will appear after the changes are made to see if more changes are necessary. They usually are because the particular changes the meaning, and the meaning influences the particular.

EDITING ACADEMIC WRITING

Remember, an academic paper is a demonstration of disciplined thought. Here is a checklist for editing the final draft of academic writing.

- *Is this house of meaning built on a solid foundation of accurate information?*
- *Are the sources of your information clear to the reader?* An academic paper is written for members of an academic community who are doing their own research, scholarship, thinking on the topic of your paper. They need to see the source of your

information not only to check its veracity but to explore those sources themselves as they investigate the topic.

- *Does your text take a critical view of the information?* Academic writing is not the accumulation of information but the product of an informed intelligence that has thought about the importance of the information. Critical does not mean negative, but it does mean have a opinion that can be supported with specific evidence.

- *Is the information in a context so its significance is clear to the reader?* The academic writer must include the environment that makes the writer's opinion worth paying attention to. That context must be clear to the reader who is inclined to snarl, "So what?" The effective academic answers the "So what?"

- *Is the meaning of the text developed in a logical, objective manner?* The reader of an academic paper expects to see the writer's thinking in process. The reader wants to examine the construction of the writer's thesis, step by step, each point growing out of the last point.

- *Are the reader's questions anticipated and answered?* All readers are engaged in a dialogue with the writers they read, but this is especially true of the members of the academic community who read actively, engaging in an process of intellectual interaction with the writer.

- *Is the voice appropriate to the topic and its readers?* Voice, the music of discourse, is usually more detached than personal writing, but it varies according to the topic and the audience. Still, an academic voice is a writer's voice tuned to the purpose of the text and its potential readers. Voice reveals the person behind the text, and the sense of an individual writer is as important in academic writing as it is in any genre.

- *Is the final draft clear? Does it break the conventions of writing only when that increases the clarity and grace of the text?* Good writing is good writing in any genre. Academic writing should have the energy, grace, humor, clarity—above all, clarity—of writing in any form. Nothing should get between the mind of the reader and the mind of the writer as they, together, confront the topic.

....

A STUDENT CASE HISTORY

It is the ultimate compliment when I work through a young writer's paper line by line. Many students want this attention, but there are reasons not to do it most of the time.

One, you can't do an effective job of line-by-line editing of your own draft—or anyone else's—unless the writer has something to say that is worth saying. As novelist and writing teacher Wallace Stegner said, "You can't sharpen a knife on a wheel of cheese."

Two, I do not know the writer's subject, and my editing must be based on understanding what the student has written, and what the student has known but left out. Most writing is left out in the sense that good writing grows from abundant soil, and I am fearful I will take the piece of writing away from the student as I edit it, inevitably, to my vision of the student's world. For example, Roger LePage's fine piece here describes the Rollinsford, New Hampshire, dump. I live nearby but have never been to that dump. I do not have the specific details in my notebook and my memory from which effective writing is constructed. I do not have Roger's vision of this world, and I do not have his way of using our language. There is a conflict here: I want Roger to see one professional writer at work on his prose, but I fear I will appropriate his prose and make it mine.

And when I do edit line by line, I am always fearful the student will take me too seriously. I tend to do this with only the best, most resistant students. The student who slavishly follows my editing will learn nothing; the student who questions what I have done and how I have done it may learn a great deal.

THE STUDENT'S ORIGINAL DRAFT

• THE DUMP •
Roger LePage, Jr.

Summer days in Rollinsford, New Hampshire were very boring until we discovered the dump. As ten-year-olds we didn't have summer jobs—except, of course, finding amusement and adventure. We didn't even do that well until the time one of us, maybe me, maybe one of the others, steered his bike off of Main Street and led the pack onto the dirt dump road. The intriguing pillar of smoke that was perpetually rising above the trees from the dump may have drawn us in. Or it could have been the "NO TRESPASSING" sign and the locked gate—things like that always invited us into abandoned houses. Whatever the reason, we discovered the dump and were not bored for the rest of the summer.

That first day we didn't even make it into the actual dump. The dirt road leading in was about half a mile long, and about half way down that we discovered a slimy little pond with lots of frogs and snakes around its fringe. We spent most of the day hunting them and trying to catch them. This didn't hold its appeal too long for me though. One of my friends, Jason, was very cruel and whenever he caught a frog he would first put it on the road and torment it with a stick, and then he would pick it up and squeeze it to death in his hand and throw the guts at whoever was within range. I was made target twice and decided it was time to go home.

But soon we made it past all the distractions along the road, which were many, including the rusting corpses of several kitchen appliances and one time there was the ass end of a deer the stench of which was still strong for a quarter mile radius. But nothing could be compared to the adventures found in the dump itself. We began in the huge pile of discarded tires, immediately abandoning our bikes right in front of it and trying to race to the top. "King of Tire Mountain" lasted for weeks, producing many bruises and scuffles and many hurt feelings. Then we built forts within the inner depths of Tire Mountain—a much more peaceful game. When it was time to try to furnish our forts we began exploring the junk in the rest of the dump.

That was when we discovered the greatest thing possible in a ten year old boy's mind: dirty magazines. I'm not sure who discovered them first, but there was soon a huge uproar and race to see who could collect and hoard the most. We would bring them back to our forts and pile them up, going through each one with great enthusiasm. We would organize them according to their appeal to us: the ones with girls showing everything spread out and accessible were our favorites, the ones with boys and girls were second, the plain boob shots were last. We had another pile of "girls with girls" which we didn't know how to take but spent most time looking at. We would move around in funny ways, always moving around to maximize that great new ache in our pants while looking at the magazines, and we all seemed to have the shakes.

***

I would also go to the dump on Saturday mornings with my dad. It was part of our Saturday morning errands: the dump, the barbers, the grocery store, then church. Most of the time he didn't even have anything to throw away. It was a Saturday morning meeting place for the true Rollinsford men—those who still called the town Salmon Falls, and a group to which my dad belongs because he was born and raised there. It was also a place of refuge from their wives: Friday night was poker night (I could always hear the door slam from my bedroom when my dad stumbled in just before day-break,) and on Saturday morning the men were red-eyed and "in the dog house" as they put it.

But my dad would go to the dump mainly to pay his respects to the toothless old Greek who I've only heard referred to as The Greek, and who was a great drinking partner of my dad's father. The Greek worked there. He made sure you didn't put metals or combustibles in with the burnables and he took his job very seriously. He tended the fire and if you tried to interfere, his toothless smile would disappear and he would straightway banish you. Banishment from the dump is one of the lowest dishonors in our town.

You wouldn't think anyone would be overly enthusiastic about being friends with the man who tends the dump, but in towns like mine occupation is not nearly as socially relevant as age or drinking ability. There were other reasons why The Greek was respected: he did once have an occupation, but he retired and instead of sitting around all day, or bagging groceries in some supermarket, he opted to tend the dump. That choice was respectable and The Greek knew this and took his job very seriously. Also he was a great old drinker and fighter, actually legendary. His missing teeth were the proof. Everybody knew that "he got them knocked out" in a fight years back. The important thing was that "he got them knocked out," not "somebody knocked his teeth out" because the latter would imply The Greek was not in control at the time. And even though it was rumored that his wife, also something of a drinker and fighter herself, has his tooth marks on her knuckles The Greek was still respected; he earned the right to be toothless. He brandished this honor too, by smiling all the time—but I never thought The Greek was such a happy man.

After my friends and I started spending so much time in the dump I began to look at the Saturday morning visits with my dad in a new way. I fancied myself a spy, watching our forts as inconspicuously as possible and always listening for clues to find out if anyone was on to us. I thought that sometimes The Greek would catch me looking at the tire pile and possibly know our secret, but I wasn't sure. I felt that it was just strange that he looked at me at all, because before my friends and I started playing at the dump The Greek never seemed to notice me. I thought then, that maybe I just never noticed him noticing me before because it wouldn't have mattered if he did. Whatever the case, I was wary.

***

Then one day we were playing at the dump, alternating between culling our dirty magazines and our next best discovery: combustibles. It was Jason, the sadistic frog squisher who discovered this one, I'm sure, he was fond of destruction in any form. On one of his devilish whims, he threw a paint can into the dump fire and silently waited for something to happen. The rest of us were busy going through junk and exploring and didn't even notice. The explosion sent us running for cover, yelling all of the profanities we knew (most of which we got out of our new magazine collection,) and nearly pissing our pants. When we realized what had taken place, the excitement of the whole thing brought us together giggling, wrestling and rolling around in the dirt. This was probably why we didn't hear the pick-up coming down the dump road.

When we did finally notice it, it had pulled up right beside us. We all jumped to our feet and stood there, not sure what to do. I recognized the green, rusty, beat up old thing—it was The Greek's truck. He got out and stared at us with full blown adult contempt, "What are you kids doing? You the ones been down here vandalizing?"

Even at ten I wondered how the hell anybody could vandalize a dump, but as I said, The Greek took his job very seriously.

"Aren't you Roger's boy? I knew I'd catch you down here," he stared at me with his exaggerated toothless frown and shook his head. His nose looked like a spoiled piece of fruit. "There's nothing but piss and vinegar running through your veins. I know. Knew your grandfather, same thing. Your dad too," he was still staring and shaking his head, the loose flaps of his jaw skin shook around violently. "I knew I'd catch you down here. How would you like me to tell your old man what you've been doing?"

No ten year old wants his parents to know what he does on summer afternoons; it's a child's first glimpse of independence and the privacy is treasured, locked away in the child's heart. When one comes along and tries to adulterate that treasure, as adults always do, the loss of the treasure is a far greater tragedy than any thought of impending punishment. I asked him meekly, "Please don't tell." The Greek looked at me and then at my companions. He turned and walked along the dirt towards Tire Mountain. I thought I was going to be sick. The Greek knew! He was on to us. First we would be banished from the dump, then from our homes and then we would be kicked out of the town altogether. Maybe even sent to prison or reform school.

"How would your mothers feel if they knew you were looking at those kinds of things?"

Oh God! I thought. It's one thing to lose your cherished summer freedom, or even to be locked away, but to have your mother think you're a pervert, to have her think you are one of those weirdos like fat old Slow Jimmy who smiles at you funny and always asks you to go for a walk. To have your mother know you look at dirty magazines! It was absolutely the worst thing imaginable.

The Greek paused and looked around. He looked at me hard. I'm sure he could see I was about to commit the unspeakable in front of my friends—that I was about to cry. He had done his job, and done it well. The Greek took his job very seriously. "Well if I catch any of you kids here again, your parents will all get a call from me. And if I catch you here again LePage, I'll give you a beating myself."

So we pedalled the hell out of there, still shaken and guilty. We resolved never to return to the dump, and we didn't ... at least for the rest of the week. But after all, as kids we also took our jobs very seriously.

A PROFESSIONAL'S EDITING

I find this a good rite-of-passage piece about an interesting and mysterious place that has depth and texture: children setting out in the world, beginning to have secret life apart from parents; a son's relationship to his father; the boy's tense relationship with Jason, the cruel leader of the boys; the narrative of their explorations of the world; The Greek, his history and status and what it means. And the writing is good, full of potential as well as wordiness and the unevenness of language expected from a beginning writer.

I thought he was ready to learn from what one writer might do to his draft. Primarily, I was interested in cutting, in clearing away the underbrush and revealing the good writing hidden by it.

I was aware of the danger that I would take over the piece and make his vision and his voice mine. I hoped he would be strong and wise enough to resist me.

In going over this for the book, I have not changed my editing, which was done quickly for purpose of instruction and in a spirit of play: "I wonder what would happen if I ... ?" I have also realized how limited my editing was because I did not want to overwhelm the writer. I would edit myself more severely, and if I was editing the piece for publication I also would have caught all sorts of things I let go.

Go back and edit Roger LePage's piece yourself alone or with a partner. Try to edit so that you reveal *his* vision of the world and free *his* voice from the draft. Work slowly with pen in hand. When you are finished compare your editing with mine.

• THE DUMP •
Roger LePage, Jr.

(very makes it less somehow)

~~Summer days in Rollinsford, New Hampshire were very boring until we discovered the dump. As ten year olds we didn't have summer jobs except, of course, finding amusement and adventure. We didn't even do that well until the time one of us, maybe me, maybe one of the others, steered his bike off of Main Street and led the pack onto the dirt dump road.~~ The ~~intriguing~~ pillar of *(a Rollinsford, New Hampshire)* smoke that was perpetually rising above the trees from the dump *(great image: smoke)* *(you say it better at the end of the sentence)* may have drawn us in. Or it could have been the "NO TRESPASSING" sign and the locked gate—things like that always invited us into abandoned houses. Whatever ~~the reason, we discovered~~ the town *were 10 years old, had a summer out of school, and where everything abandoned was new, full of possibility.* dump ~~and were not bored for the rest of the summer.~~

(Too many flat statements – draw us in as you have below.)

Th~~at~~e first day we didn't even make it into the actual dump. The dirt road leading in was about half a mile long, and about half way down that we discovered a slimy little pond with ~~lots of~~ *(wonderful word)* frogs and snakes around its fringe. We spent most of the day hunting, ~~them and~~ trying to catch them. ~~This didn't hold its appeal too long for me though. One of my friends,~~ *But when* Jason, ~~was very cruel and whenever he~~ caught a frog he would first put it on the road and torment it with a stick, ~~and~~ then he would pick it up and squeeze it to death in ~~his~~ *one* hand and throw the guts at whoever was within range. I was ~~made~~ *the* target twice and ~~decided it~~ *took off for* ~~was time to go~~ home.

But ~~soon~~ *another day* we made it past ~~all the distractions along the road, which were many, including~~ the rusting corpses of several *(what were they?)* kitchen appliances and ~~one time there was~~ the ass end of a deer, ~~the stench of which was still strong~~ *with a stench that followed us* for a quarter mile ~~radius.~~ ~~But~~ *But when we arrived at the dump we* ~~nothing could be compared to the adventures found in the dump itself.~~ We began in the huge pile of discarded tires, ~~immediately~~ abandon~~ing~~*ed* our bikes ~~right in front of it~~ and ~~trying~~ *tried* to race to the top. "King of Tire Mountain" lasted for weeks, ~~producing many bruises and scuffles and many hurt feelings.~~ Then we built forts

(don't keep telling us, show)

(watch out for ings)

within the inner depths of Tire Mountain, ~~a much more peaceful game.~~ When it was time to try to furnish our forts we ~~began~~ explor~~ing~~ed the junk in the rest of the dump.

That was when we discovered ~~the greatest thing possible in a ten-year-old boy's mind,~~ dirty magazines. ~~I'm not sure who discovered them first, but there was soon a huge uproar and race to see who could collect and hoard the most.~~ We ~~would bring~~ lugged them back to our forts and ~~pile them up, going through each one with great enthusiasm. We would~~ organize them, ~~according to their appeal to us:~~ the ones with girls showing everything spread out ~~and accessible were our favorites,~~ were first, the ones with boys and girls ~~were~~ second, ~~the~~ plain boob shots were last. We had another pile of 'girls with girls' which we didn't know how to take but spent the most time looking at. We ~~would~~ moved around ~~in funny ways, always moving around~~ to maximize that ~~great~~ new ache in our pants while looking at the magazines, and we all seemed to have the shakes.

(watch out for would)   ***

I ~~would~~ also ~~go~~ went to the dump on Saturday mornings with my dad. ~~It was part of our Saturday morning errands:~~ the dump, the barbers, the grocery store, then church. Most of the time he didn't even have anything to throw away. It was a Saturday morning meeting place for the ~~true~~ Rollinsford men ~~those~~ who still called the town Salmon Falls, and ~~a group to which my dad belongs because he was~~ were born and raised there. It was also a place of refuge from their wives: Friday night was poker night (I could always hear the door slam from my bedroom when my dad stumbled in just before day-break), and on Saturday morning the men were red-eyed and "in the dog house" as they put it.

~~But~~ my dad ~~would go~~ went to the dump mainly to pay his respects to the toothless old Greek, ~~who I've only heard referred to as The Greek, and who was~~ a great drinking partner of my dad's father. The Greek ~~worked there. He~~ made sure you didn't put metals or combustibles in with the burnables and he took his job very seriously. He tended the fire and if you tried to interfere, his toothless smile would disappear and he would ~~straightway~~ banish you. Banishment from the dump is ~~one of~~ the ~~lowest~~ greatest dishonors in our town.

~~You wouldn't think anyone would be overly enthusiastic about being friends with the man who tends the dump, but in towns like mine, occupation is not nearly as socially relevant as age or drinking ability. There were other reasons why~~ The Greek was respected; [because when] ~~he did once have an occupation, but~~ he retired [(from what?)] ~~and instead of~~ [he didn't] sitting around all day, or bagging groceries [at the] ~~in some~~ supermarket, [but took control of] ~~he opted to tend~~ the dump. ~~That choice was respectable and The Greek knew this and took his job very seriously. Also~~ [he] was a great old drinker and fighter, actually [legendary] ~~His~~ missing teeth were ~~the proof. Everybody knew that 'he got them~~ "knocked out" in a fight years back. The important thing was that "he got them knocked out," not "somebody knocked his teeth out" because the latter would imply The Greek was not in control at the time. ~~And even though~~ it was rumored that his wife, also something of a drinker and fighter herself, has his tooth marks on her knuckles. ~~The Greek was still respected; he~~ earned the right to be toothless. He brandished this honor too, by smiling all the time—but I never thought The Greek was ~~such~~ a happy man. ⟶

(next paragraph great — puts all this in a deeper context — a stage of growing and growing away from a parent)

After my friends and I started spending so much time in the dump I began to look at the Saturday morning visits with my dad in a new way. I fancied myself a spy, watching our forts as inconspicuously as possible and always listening for clues to find out if anyone was on to us. I thought that sometimes The Greek would catch me looking at the tire pile and possibly know our secret, but I wasn't sure. I felt that it was just strange that he looked at me at all, because before my friends and I started playing at the dump, The Greek never seemed to notice me. I thought then, that maybe I just never noticed him noticing me before because it wouldn't have mattered if he did. Whatever the case, I was wary.

***

~~Then~~ one day we were playing at the dump, alternating between culling our dirty magazines and our next best discovery: combustibles. It was Jason, [of course, who] ~~the sadistic frog squisher who discovered this one, I'm sure; he was fond~~ of ~~destruction in any form. On one of his devilish whims, he~~ threw a paint can into the dump fire and ~~silently~~ waited for something to happen. The rest of us were busy going through junk and exploring and didn't even notice. The explosion sent us running for cover, yelling all of the profanities we knew, (most of which we got out of our new magazine collection) ~~and nearly pissing our pants.~~ When we realized what ~~had taken place,~~ *Jason had done,* the excitement ~~of the whole thing~~ brought us together giggling, wrestling and rolling around in the dirt. ~~This was probably why~~ we didn't hear the pick-up coming down the dump road.

~~When we did finally notice it,~~ it ~~had~~ pulled up right beside us, *and* ~~We all~~ jumped to our feet, ~~and stood there,~~ not sure what to do. *(Plymouth, Ford, what?)* I recognized the green, rusty, beat up old thing—it was The Greek's truck. He got out and stared at us with ~~full blown adult~~ contempt, "~~What are you kids doing?~~ You the ones been down here vandalizing?"

Even at ten I wondered how the hell anybody could *be* vandalizing a dump, but ~~as I said,~~ The Greek took his job ~~very~~ seriously.

"Aren't you Roger's boy? I knew I'd catch you down here," he stared at me with his exaggerated toothless frown and shook his head. His nose looked like a spoiled piece of fruit. "There's nothing but piss and vinegar running through your veins. I know. Knew your grandfather, same thing. Your dad too," he was still staring and shaking his head, the loose flaps of his jaw skin shook around violently. "I knew I'd catch you down here. How would you like me to tell your old man what you've been doing?"

No ten-year-old wants his parents to know what he does on summer afternoons; ~~it's a child's first glimpse of independence and the privacy is treasured, locked away in the child's heart. When one comes along and tries to adulterate that treasure, as adults always do, the loss of the treasure is a far greater tragedy than any thought of impending punishment.~~ I asked him, ~~meekly,~~ "Please don't tell."

The Greek looked at me and then at my companions. He turned and walked along the dirt towards Tire Mountain. ~~I thought I was going to be sick.~~ The Greek knew! He was on to us. First we would be banished from the dump, then from our homes and then we would be kicked out of the town altogether. Maybe even sent to prison or reform school.

"How would your mothers feel if they knew you were looking at those kinds of things?"

Oh God! I thought. ~~It's one thing to lose your cherished summer freedom, or even to be locked away, but to have your~~

~~mother think you're a pervert,~~ to have ~~her~~ **Mother** think you are ~~one of those weirdos~~ like fat old Slow Jimmy who smiles at you funny and always asks you to go for a walk. To have your mother know you look at dirty magazines! ~~It was absolutely the worst thing imaginable.~~

The Greek paused and looked around. He looked at me hard. I'm sure he could see I was about to ~~commit the unspeakable in front of my friends —that I was about to~~ cry. ~~He had done his job, and done it well. The Greek took his job very seriously.~~ "Well, if I catch any of you kids here again, your parents will all get a call from me. And if I catch you here again LePage, I'll give you a beating myself."

~~So we pedalled the hell out of there, still shaken and guilty.~~ We ~~resolved never to~~ **didn't** return to the dump ~~and we didn't . . . at least~~ for ~~the rest of the~~ **a** week. ~~But after all, as kids we also took our jobs very seriously.~~

THE STUDENT'S REACTION TO PROFESSIONAL EDITING

The good writing student will listen to what the readers of his drafts have to say—fellow writers, instructors, editors—but will resist when necessary. LePage reacted strongly to my line-by-line editing:

I'll start off with the problem I had with the revised story, just to get it out of the way. The first thing I did when I received your edited version of my draft was to rewrite the story using all of your suggestions. Then I read it aloud over and over, and something just didn't sound right. I have no specific examples of the revisions which caused this, but some element seemed to be missing. I was down to the bare essentials of the story, the skeleton. The problem with this, as I see it, is all skeletons look alike. It's the flesh that gives the narration character.

I'll use Raymond Carver as an example. He is sometimes referred to as a "minimalist" (as I'm sure you know) because at first glance his stories appear to be whittled down to skeleton form. However, that is not completely the case. He adds the flesh to the narration where it is necessary and he does it in such a way that the narrator, whether first person or not, booms with personality. For example, in the excellent story "Cathedral," Carver describes a meal in this way: "We dug in.

We ate everything there was to eat on the table. We ate like there was no tomorrow. We didn't talk. We ate. We scarfed. We grazed that table. We were into serious eating." I don't know any editors, but I would guess that most would pull their hair out over a passage like this. There is unnecessary repetition and clichés. But what's great about it is we are allowed to understand the narrator: he is a regular guy with a good sense of humor and a natural joy for life. We understand this only because Carver knows how and when to break the rules, and he knows how his narrator is supposed to sound.

So I had to make the story sound right to me. When I talk about sound, I think I'm talking about voice, but I'm not sure. My idea of sound is this: when you're sitting at your writing desk and reading your work aloud and the person in the next room doesn't ask what you're reading from, but who your talking to, then it's good. I think this is the most important element in a story, that it sounds right. The second would be that you have a good story to tell.

What the revisions did was help to make my story move. I'm learning slowly, mostly as I gain confidence and experience, that I don't need to reinforce every point I have shown through anecdote or image by stating it explicitly. Phrases such as "a much more peaceful game," not only slow the story down but insult the reader. Other phrases like, "the greatest thing possible in a ten year old boy's mind," cause a similar problem. For one thing, I might be alienating some readers who may not have been, at ten years old, so enthusiastic to see dirty magazines as I was. Further, even if all ten year olds do share this interest, there is no need for me to state it. I'm getting between the reader and the story. I am inserting an annoying little voice that whispers over the reader's ear and tells him how to feel and what to think, just in case my narrator is not doing his job.

The way I originally opened the story was also a sort of distraction in that it bored the reader, rather than engaging his interest. Instead of flatly stating that we were bored and the dump was exciting, it is much better to open with the same image that attracted us into the dump: the pillar of smoke. The reader will then pick up on our journey right at the exact *point where we began and join us in discovering the source of the smoke. The reader needs to "see" what we saw, the actual scene, not some filtered, transmuted secondhand account of it. The idea of voice is still pertinent here, though it's much more subtle, almost subliminal. It's the idea that the reader becomes subconsciously aware of the person, the personality, telling the story and will pass judgment on that personality just as on any other stranger. Whether the reader likes or dislikes this personality is irrelevant; what matters is that the reader trusts him. The only way I know to make the reader trust my narration is to tell the truth, pimples and all. If a Freudian were to get a hold of this piece and make conclusions about me or my upbringing, so be it. I had to tell it like it is.*

I also had problems describing The Greek. Aside from the flat statement similar to those that opened the story, and aside from the annoying little voice that tried to dictate how the reader should feel about The Greek, I created a kind of refrain with, "The Greek took his job very seriously." The technique could work, I believe, but only if the story was centrally about this character. My story did not center around The Greek but around a group of ten year old boys and for this reason a refrain about The Greek is misleading.

Lastly, my concluding paragraph was originally too drawn out, and like the opening paragraph, too flat. The fact is, we were afraid, embarrassed and anxious to flee, but all that should be obvious. Again, I don't need to state it. The only problem with the revised ending was that it didn't sound right. It was too abrupt. I had to find a medium point that kept the rhythm of the piece, sounded right, yet didn't give the reader the urge to skip over it.

My worry now is that in correcting old mistakes I have created new ones. I don't know if I'll ever in my life be able to say, "Okay, this is done."

That is an ideal example of a student response. He pays attention and learns but makes up his mind. It is, after all, his essay.

THE STUDENT'S REVISION

• THE DUMP •
Roger LePage, Jr.

The pillar of smoke that perpetually rose above the trees into a puffy gray cloud over the Rollinsford, New Hampshire, dump may have drawn us in. Or it could have been the "NO TRESPASSING" sign and the locked gate—things like that always invited us into abandoned houses. As ten-year-olds out of school for the summer we only wanted to be where we shouldn't or where the possibility of adventure seemed fullest. The town dump was to become our spot.

The first day we didn't even make it into the actual dump. The dirt road leading in was about half a mile long, and about halfway down that we discovered a slimy little pond with lots of frogs and snakes around its fringe. We spent most of the day hunting, trying to catch them. But that eventually stopped being fun, at least for me, because when Jason caught a frog he would first put it on the road and torment it with a stick, then he would pick up the frog and squeeze it to death in one hand and throw the guts at whoever was in range. I was the target twice and took off for home.

But another day we made it past all the rusting corpses of stoves, refrigerators and washer machines and even past the ass end of a deer with a stench that seemed to linger around us for at least a quarter mile. When we got into the dump, we first came upon the huge pile of discarded tires and immediately ditched our bikes right in front of it and raced to the top. "King of Tire Mountain" lasted for weeks, and each day when we became too bruised and tired for that game, we built forts within the inner depths of the mountain. When it was time to try to furnish our forts we headed for the junk in the rest of the dump.

That was when we discovered dirty magazines. There was a huge race to see who could collect and hoard the most. We hurried them back to our forts and then organized them: the ones with girls showing everything spread out was the first pile, the ones with boys and girls was second, plain boob shots were last.

We had another pile of "girls with girls" which we didn't know how to take but spent the most time looking at. We lay down on our stomachs to look at them, maximizing that new ache in our pants, and we all seemed to have the shakes.

***

I also went to the dump on Saturday mornings with my dad: the dump, the barbers, the grocery store, then church. Most of the time he didn't even have anything to throw away. It was a Saturday morning meeting place for the Rollinsford men—those who still called the town Salmon Falls and were born and raised there. It was also a place of refuge from their wives: Friday night was poker night (I could always hear the door slam from my bedroom when my dad stumbled in just before day break), and on Saturday morning the men were red-eyed and "in the dog house" as they put it.

My dad went to the dump mainly to pay his respects to the toothless old Greek, a drinking partner of my dad's father. The Greek made sure that you didn't put metals or combustibles in with the burnables and he took his job seriously. He tended the fire and if you tried to interfere, his toothless smile would disappear and he would banish you. Banishment from the dump is the greatest dishonor in our town.

The Greek was respected because when he retired from the railroad he didn't sit around all day or bag groceries at the supermarket, He took over the dump. Also he was a legendary old drinker and fighter. His missing teeth were "knocked out" in a fight years back. The important thing was that "he got them knocked out," not "somebody knocked his teeth out" because the latter would imply that The Greek was not in control at the time. It was rumored that his wife, also something of a drinker and fighter herself, had his tooth marks on her knuckles. But he earned the right to be toothless. And he brandished this honor too, by smiling all the time—though I never thought for a minute The Greek was a happy man.

After my friends and I started spending so much time in the dump I began to look at the Saturday morning visits with my dad in a new way. I was no longer a mere tag-along, I had a need to be there of my own—a mission. I was not a child by my father's side, but a grown man, a spy watching our forts as inconspicuously as possible and always listening for clues to find out if anyone was on to us. I thought that sometimes The Greek would catch me looking at the tire pile and possibly know our secret, but I wasn't sure. I felt that it was just strange that he looked at me at all, because before my friends and I started playing at the dump The Greek never seemed to notice me. This, I decided, was because of my new identity: a man (even if he is a spy) automatically earns another's notice. But just in case, I remained wary.

***

One day when we were playing at the dump, alternating between culling our dirty magazines and exploring the junk piles, we came upon our next best discovery: combustibles. It was Jason, of course, who threw a paint can into the dump fire and waited for something to happen. The rest of us were too engrossed in the junk to notice. The explosion sent us running for cover, yelling all of the profanities we knew—most of which we got out of our new magazines collection. When we realized what Jason had done, the excitement heaved us together giggling, wrestling and rolling around in the dirt. We didn't hear the pickup coming down the dump road.

It pulled up right beside me and we jumped to our feet, not sure what to do. I recognized the green, rusty, beat up old "Ford"—it was The Greek's truck. He got out and stared at us with contempt. "You the ones been down here vandalizing?"

Even at ten I wondered how the hell anybody could vandalize a dump. The Greek did take his job seriously.

"Aren't you Roger's boy? I knew I'd catch you down here," he stared at me with his exaggerated toothless frown and shook his head. His nose looked like a spoiled piece of fruit. "There's nothing but piss and vinegar running through your veins. I know. Knew your grandfather, same thing. Your dad too." He was still staring and shaking his head, the loose flaps of his jaw skin shook around violently. "I knew I'd catch you down here. How would you like me to tell your old man what you've been doing?"

No ten year old wants his parents to know what he does on summer afternoons. I asked him, "Please don't tell."

The Greek looked at me and my companions. He turned and walked along the dirt towards Tire Mountain. The Greek knew! He was on to us. First we would be banished from the dump, then from our homes and then we would be kicked out of the town altogether. Maybe even sent to prison or reform school.

"How would your mothers' feel if they knew you were looking at those things?"

Oh God! I thought. To have your mother think you're like fat, old Slow Jimmy who smiles at you funny and always asks you to go for a walk. To have her know you look at dirty magazines!

The Greek paused and looked around. He looked at me hard. I'm sure he could see I was about to cry. "If I catch any of you kids here again, your parents will all get a call from me. And if I catch you here again LePage, I'll give you a beating myself."

We scrambled for our bikes never to return again, and we didn't—for the rest of the week anyway.

....

DOES REVISION EVER END?

Revision is a game the writer plays for life. Roger LePage says, "I don't know if I'll ever in my life be able to say, 'OK, this is done,'" and years earlier the French poet Paul Valéry said, "A poem is never finished, only abandoned."

I heard despair in such quotations when I was as young as Roger LePage, but I now feel excitement and opportunity. This edition of *The Craft of Revision* is greatly different from the last one. I don't know if it is better—I hope so—but it is different. After more than 50 years of rewriting, I have learned from this draft. It is finished—abandoned—only because of the deadline. Writing inspires writing, and I treasure the fact that each morning as I come to my writing desk, mystery and surprise await. My bones may creak, but as a writer I am forever young, forever learning as I write and rewrite.

CHAPTER 9

REWRITE AT WORK

In school you have had the opportunity to explore your world by writing and rewriting personal experience papers. You have been trained to report the results of academic investigation from within the laboratory, the library, and the community by writing research reports and term papers. You've also developed critical skills by writing papers of academic argument and opinion. All those academic skills can be applied to the workplace.

A few years ago, a study revealed that after graduation engineers did more writing than English majors. The need for effective communication at work continues to increase. The international corporation is common. Our world has shrunk so that corporations and governments must be in touch with each other on a daily, sometimes an hourly basis.

The demand to write—and rewrite—gives us a chance to learn on the job. We learn best when we have to describe or explain using the discipline of written language. Our ignorance is revealed by the draft. We discover what we know and what we need to know and, by rewriting, we come to know it.

The critical skills we have honed in the classroom are vital on the job. We have to read sales marketing reports, social workers' cases, engineering design proposals, legal briefs and write critical responses pointing out strengths and weaknesses, asking the tough questions that must be asked.

Writing in the workplace can also bring the writer influence and power. Writing has a much greater impact than an oral report. Writing demands attention, and its influence can extend far beyond the office in which the writer works.

You will find that the intellectual training you have had in college has prepared you for the workplace. The book review, the hour exam, the research paper, the critical essay all have, under different names, a place in the world of work. Once you start doing on-the-job writing, you will find most of the tasks familiar.

And how do I, a writer and former English professor, know about writing in the workplace? Most writers lead double or triple lives. I have ghosted a piece of writing for a governor, ghosted pieces for cabinet officials and corporate executives, and helped earn the money for my daughter's college tuition serving as a freelance writer for the CEO of a national corporation. And as a college professor, English Department chairperson, and member of too many committees, I have written the papers, recommendations, proposals, and reports that make a university run.

TIPS FOR COMPLETING COMMON WORKPLACE WRITING TASKS

As you begin a new job, you will face certain writing tasks. Make notes as you write, rewrite, and respond to the reader's reaction so that you have a helpful resource when the task is assigned again.

REWRITE TO DEADLINE

All writing at work will be to deadline, and there will be few extensions. Miss a deadline and you may find yourself looking for a new job. And most deadlines will be unreasonable. It is important to develop strategies to deal with delivery dates that can't be met and must.

Situation

The new product proposal scheduled for the April 15 board of directors' meeting is going to be considered at the January 18 meeting. It is January 4 and the head of new products assigns the report to you.

Solution

Break the assignment down so you have achievable daily tasks as you did when completing a term paper in European history. Make a schedule backward from the board of directors' meeting:

Monday, January 18: Board meeting.

Friday, January 15: Print new product proposal.

Thursday, January 14: Final edit.

Wednesday, January 13: Sign off for final copy by head of new products and all who are involved.

Tuesday, January 12: ⎱ Write.
Monday, January 11: ⎰ Final draft.

Friday, January 8: Keep drafting and chasing down information needed for final report.

Thursday, January 7: Start drafting descriptions of new products. Chase down late descriptions.

Wednesday, January 6: Write early. Start drafting any section possible. Chase down new product descriptions.

Tuesday, January 5: Outline new product presentation. Design format.

Monday, January 4: List the new products that are to be proposed. Confirm with head of new products. Request detailed description of each product by Wednesday noon.

Other Tips

- Refocus the task, limiting the assignment so that it can be completed by the deadline. The published writer usually seeks strict limits: not the universe but the neighborhood; not the neighbors but an individual; not a lifetime but a single act that changed a lifetime.

- Read quickly to see what can be cut and what doesn't need to be rewritten. Focus on what can *not* be cut and must be revised.
- Do only what you can do within the time you have. There is comfort in the possible.

REWRITE WITH A COMMITTEE

Often a committee, panel, project group, research team, or other unit will have to produce a document. The relationship of members to each other can be very complex, with each person representing his or her own interests. The result can be a great deal of talk and very little productive writing as it was when you first did collaborative writing in a literature class.

Situation

Engineering team leaders must produce a report on how the laboratory can cut its costs by 5 percent in the next fiscal year.

Solution

The person to draft the report is chosen at the first meeting. The writer asks each committee member to write down three items that might be cut and what each cut would save.

The writer produces a draft of the report and circulates it so each member can edit a specific draft before the next meeting. The members meet as often as necessary to produce a draft they can all sign.

Other Tips

- Have everyone write a paragraph describing each of the main points they want included. It takes greater discipline to write than to talk about a position.
- Start the first session by having everyone write for five minutes about what they want included. Then have each person read what they have written aloud. This will reveal where

each individual is coming from and may also reveal who should be the principal writer.

- Propose an outline at the first meeting and edit it until everyone agrees. Then assign each section to a different person with a specific length and deadline.
- Keep the committee in session for the final edit, working through it paragraph by paragraph.
- Get the committee to agree on one sentence inside or outside the draft that states the main point to be developed.

REWRITE IN RESPONSE TO CRITICISM

Writing is thinking, and most on-the-job writing involves a process of drafting in which ideas are put forth, criticized, and revised in a series of papers. Often the criticism seems personal and many times it is. Remember how you got beyond your anger at a professor with a sarcastic pen and rewrote a C paper into an A.

Situation

The assistant sales manager suggests that the emphasis on finding new customers be shifted to better serving the customers the company already has. His boss, the sales manager, and the head of the service division each take his suggestion as a personal attack and severely criticize the report.

Solution

The assistant sales manager listens to the specific criticisms, tuning out the personal attacks. He rewrites the report, pointing out that they have been successful in attracting new customers and that they have provided excellent service. Then he points out how they could increase sales by this shift of emphasis without the cost of increasing the size of the sales staff and its travel expenses, using the strength of the company that is in place.

Other Tips

- Listen carefully to the criticism. Take notes or play it back. It is easy to hear what you want to hear, hard to hear what you need to hear.

- Accept the criticism you secretly expect, the corner you tried to cut.

- Consider the criticism that surprises you the most. It usually means you have said what you did not expect to say.

- Recognize that there is not one wrong or right way; there are a thousand ways to be wrong or right. Find another of the thousand ways to be right and try it.

REWRITE FOR A DIFFERENT PURPOSE

It is common for a draft written for a specific purpose or audience to be revised for another purpose or audience. You are more experienced at this than you may think, since you have had to adapt your papers and exam writing to a series of professors who taught the same subject but had very different ideas about good writing.

Situation

The assistant sales manager's new policy with emphasis on service is adopted and he is assigned to write a "We Want to Serve You Better" brochure to be sent to each customer using the original proposal he wrote earlier.

Solution

He interviews the key people in the service department and finds they have interesting qualifications. He also finds they each see common problems that the customer could solve themselves without losing the time it takes to call in the service department.

He gets authorization to hire a desktop publishing graphics designer who helps him produce a problem-oriented booklet. The customer can look up a problem and see on one page the picture of an individual service person and read what action that person recommends before calling for service.

Other Tips

- State the new purpose in one sentence to make sure you are on target. Check that sentence with a supervisor to make sure you both are aiming at the same target.

- Reconsider the form of writing. Will the old form or genre work for the new purpose or should you choose a new form?

- List the types of information that would advance and support the new purpose.

- Read the draft aloud to see if the tone is appropriate for the new purpose.

- Now that you have a draft, a map or outline may be helpful so you can see the logic of the draft you are going to revise. It may be easy to see how a new order can serve the new purpose. Then it may be possible to clip and paste the draft in a new, effective order.

REWRITE FOR A NEW AUDIENCE

Many times a successful final draft will be redirected to a new audience. An engineering report, for example, may be important enough that it should now be seen by the company's CEO.

Situation

An internal government agency report revealed that taxpayers were losing money when used equipment was sold without bids. Now the head of the agency wants to use the report in a speech at a business convention. You've been assigned to rewrite the report.

Solution

Write down the strong points of the agency head that you have noticed when you have heard her speak. Listen to a few tapes of her making speeches and identify her most effective qualities.

Research the group she will be addressing, and also find out if she is speaking early in the morning, at a lunch or dinner, or in the late afternoon so that you can understand the difficulty she will have in keeping the attention of her audience. Identify the voice and the form that will communicate her meaning.

Redraft the report, imagining that you are the agency head appealing to this specific audience.

Other Tips

- Identify an individual you know—and respect—who represents that new audience. Read the draft from this person's point of view.
- Write down the questions a member of the audience will ask.
- Put the questions in the order the reader will ask them.
- List the forms of documentation this audience will trust.
- Identify the forms of information that will impress this audience.

REWRITE SHORT

It is common for the top executives of a corporation or a government agency to require that all reports be reduced to one page that either substitutes for the report or is used as a cover for the report itself.

Situation

A 47-page proposal for the company's new environmental hazards policy has to be reduced to a single page to be released to the press along with copies of the full report. It is Tuesday and the press conference is Thursday at 10 AM.

Solution

Pick the five or fewer most important points the way you went through a professor's lecture notes or textbook before an exam. You may even focus on one single point or a theme that runs through all of the actions. For example, Krasner Corporation will store its most hazardous waste products until methods for safely destroying them are discovered.

It is a temptation to compress too much material into the single page—the garbage compactor technique. Effective brief writing, however, is a matter of selection. The points you choose must be developed so they can be understood.

Other Tips

- Read the piece quickly and mark the sections and paragraphs that can be cut without a loss in the meaning of the draft.

- Read the draft slowly, line by line, tightening the prose so that every word counts. Make sure each sentence and each paragraph carries a full load of information to the reader. The more specific the nouns and the verbs, the more information they will carry to the reader.
- Put the report aside after rereading it, and draft a page that says the same thing. What you have left out probably needs to be left out, and what you leave in may well be what needs to be communicated.

REWRITE LONG

Sometimes it is necessary to take a brief piece of writing and develop it into a longer document as professors may have asked you to do. The professor usually didn't just want a statement—"it's a good book"—but a full report with evidence to support your position.

Situation

The hospital has reduced its admissions and discharge procedures to a simple chart for staff members. Now you have been assigned to turn it into a brochure that will be given to patients when they schedule procedures or when they are admitted.

Solution

Create a narrative of a typical patient showing that person going through the entire sequence. Once you have drafted the narrative, go through and define any terms that may confuse a patient. Then insert counsel for someone who is taking care of the patient and has to perform admission and discharge procedures for them.

Other Tips

- Write with information. Mark the points in the draft where the reader could use more evidence.
- Write a fast discovery draft to see what subconscious connections your draft will appear to make on its own. You will have to cut back later, but the velocity of the writing may reveal a richness of material that will allow you to construct a stronger, more fully realized draft.

- Vary the form of evidence—statistical, anecdotal, historical, scientific—so that it supports the point being made and serves the reader.
- Make the information even more specific and detailed.
- Develop: take the time to make the reader see and understand each point with a richness of abundant detail.

REWRITE FOR A PRESENTATION

Most organizations are constantly preparing or giving presentations. Computer programs make it easy to produce slides, handouts, and other presentation materials, but it is still the job of the writer to decide what needs to be presented and how.

Situation

Your employer, a bank, has just acquired another bank. You are assigned to develop a presentation for the new bank managers that will identify the principal procedures which will have to be changed to conform to the purchasing bank's operating methods.

Solution

Request a list of procedural conflicts from each bank department; then put the procedural changes in a process order that will make sense to the new bank managers.

Write a script for the vice president to follow as she identifies each procedural conflict and resolves it. Work with a graphics expert to develop slides that reinforce and dramatize the main points in the script.

Develop a packet to be given to each branch manager that includes the script, slides, and handouts so they can use it with their department heads and the department heads can, in turn, use it with their staff.

Other Tips

- Identify the audience and the single, most important message you want to communicate to the audience.

- Select important pieces of information that might be supported by slides, video displays, handouts.
- Pace the order of development so that you anticipate and respond to the skepticism of the audience and then make your case, vigorously and clearly, so the audience leaves with your main point in mind.
- If you are going to read your presentation, read it aloud as you edit it, seeking an effective voice that seems conversational and a pace that allows the reader to absorb each point before going on to the next one.

REWRITE FROM A PRESENTATION

Often a presentation—or a speech from notes—will be successful and the organization will decide it should be in print. If the talk has been audio or video recorded that sounds easy, but what worked with a live audience may not work in writing. The speaker is spontaneous and makes meaning clear with well-timed pauses, gesture, facial expression, and by underlining meaning with a change in speech. The writer has to create a draft based on the presentation but that is different from the spoken text.

Situation

The founder of the company made a lively presentation before stockholders at the company's tenth anniversary. The board of directors decided that the speech should be published and distributed to customers, present employees, and new employees when they are hired.

You have a week to do it and you are horrified at the assignment. You were present at the talk and realize how much the founder's powerful personality carried the day. In fact, the speech was almost illiterate in spots, confusing in others, and wrong in a few places where the founder remembers what did not happen.

Solution

Get the notes from which the founder spoke, make a photocopy, and listen to the audiotape, noting the most important points and significant phrases that provide insight on the subject or capture the flavor of his speech. Then write the draft in a way that will work on the page. (The draft is submitted to the founder who says it is exactly what he said!)

Other Tips

- Reconsider the form of the documentation. The chart that works as a slide during a presentation may not work in a written draft; the anecdote that made the audience laugh because of the inflection you gave key words and phrases may not make a reader laugh.

- The listener may allow you to build up to the main point, but the reader may not read on unless the main point is made clear early in the written text. The written text should be paced for a reader, not an audience.

- Read aloud to see if the written draft preserves the oral quality of the presentation whenever possible.

- Have a tape of the talk typed and edit it to make it clear to readers.

REWRITE IN A NEW FORM

Often we are asked to turn a term paper into a scholarly essay or a business menu into a speech. However, information that is written successfully in one form may need to be rewritten in another form to reach another audience. The text can't be wrenched around to serve each purpose but needs to be reconsidered from the beginning.

Situation

You have been handed a glowing report by an objective agency on patient care at a private mental hospital where you work. You realize the material in the report could be effective for staff members, potential financial contributors, and patients if it was presented in different forms.

Solution

Staff members might receive a letter of appreciation from the top administrator. Potential donors might be moved by case histories that document the main points in the report. Patients might be served by a brochure that anticipates and answers patients' questions.

Other Tips

- Read or scan some good examples of the new form, writing down the fundamental techniques and design of the new form.

- Make a rough fit of your draft into the new tradition; then write aloud to smooth over the rough spots and give the reader the illusion of spontaneity.

- Note what documentation does not work with the new form; note what new documentation you need to find that will fit the new form.

- Tune the voice so it is appropriate to the new form.

REWRITE SOMEONE ELSE'S DRAFT

When a draft doesn't work to the satisfaction of a manager, it will usually be given to someone else to rewrite. This is usually a difficult situation for the original writer as well as the fixer.

Situation

Your immediate supervisor has drafted a report for his manager, and now the latter calls you and says he wants you to take a run at it. He feels it lacks focus and is dull. It will never be read.

Solution

Go to your boss and tell him you have been assigned to revise his draft. He is hurt and angry but at *his* boss, not at you. Ask him for advice in writing for the manager and other suggestions about what might be added to this particular piece.

Read the draft, looking for a new focus that can be established in the first paragraph and woven through the report. Then make each point with specific information. Specifics are the key to liveliness.

Other Tips

- Work within the point of view of the author if possible.
- Read quickly to discover the strongest points in the draft.
- Develop those points. Then, if necessary, add additional points.
- If you can, try to use the language and the voice of the author. Help the writer be the writer; don't try to make it your piece.

REWRITE TO APPLY FOR SUPPORT

Many organizations and agencies, as well as units within the corporation, depend on support from potential contributors who receive many such appeals. Writing for support is a year-round task for science labs, social welfare organizations, schools, and hospitals as they ask for support from foundations, corporations, government agencies.

Situation

You are an English teacher in a high school who has been increasingly disturbed that many students with potential are dropping out of school. You tell your principal that you were a dropout yourself and you would like to teach an evening class for dropouts. Now he calls you in, offers his support, and assigns you to write a proposal for your district's conservative school board.

Solution

You remember how you learned to write applications for admission to college and graduate school as well as all the scholarship application essays you wrote. You accept the orientation of the school board members who are not going to be sympathetic to dropouts, imagining purple mohawks and hard drugs.

You decide to write a fiscal appeal, getting information from other cities where dropouts have gotten off public welfare rolls and begun to earn their way—and pay taxes. You prepare a chart that shows the cost of the program and projects it will return more money to the community than it costs in four years.

Other Tips

- If there are instructions from the organization or person who can offer support, read them carefully. Many grants, for example, demand a specific form and require specific evidence of need. Follow the instructions.
- Brainstorm the reasons you need support.
- Outline the reasons in an order that will apply to the proposal's reader.
- Be specific. Concrete details that document the work that has been done and that needs to be done are persuasive. The more accurate and revealing the details, the more effective the case.
- Do not assume that the reader knows your work or its quality. Document in a professional manner what you have done and what detached observers have thought of it.
- Do not argue; just present your case and let the evidence argue for you.
- Provide supporting documents, biographies, letters of support in a manner that makes it easy for readers to find information.

REWRITE TO EVALUATE SOMEONE

In the workplace there is a constant flow of personnel evaluations and recommendations, and the further you progress in any organization—school, church, health care, government agency, business—the more evaluations and recommendations you will have to write.

Situation

You have to write a yearly evaluation of the five people in your department. Salary increases will depend in part on these recommendations, and there are rumors the department may be cut, so jobs may be on the line.

Solution

You collect—from memory and from the records—specific contributions that each person has made during the year. You know that vague, general statements of support will not help the candidate. Evidence is what your superiors need. You write reports with accurate, detailed information in an objective tone, allowing the record to speak for itself.

Other Tips

- If there are guidelines, read and follow them.
- Pick the candidate's strongest quality and show how that quality will fit the job.
- Be specific, and never assume those who read the recommendation will know what the person you are recommending has done.
- Put the person's work in a professional context so the reader who may not know the field in which the candidate is working will understand the significance of what the candidate has done.
- Be honest. It is not fair to the candidate, to the person who may hire or support the candidate, or to you to create a mythical candidate.

REWRITE TO PROMOTE YOURSELF

Writing job applications is just the beginning. In most jobs you will have to write self-evaluations and proposals for transfer to new jobs or for promotion.

Situation

You have been working in the engineering division, and a new job selling the product you've helped develop opens up. You'd like to try sales, so you write a letter applying for the job.

Solution

You make a point of your familiarity with the product and the fact you have been an engineering team leader for five years, evidence that you know how to work with people. You add that you have done a survey of the potential buyers, 80 percent have engineering degrees, and you know how to talk to engineers.

Other Tips

- Read the guidelines and follow them.
- Neither be overly modest nor argue for yourself. Give the reader the detailed evidence of what you have done and how it has been received.
- Put your work in the context of the professional world in which it has been performed.
- Do not make an appeal. Give the reader the evidence that will make the reader support you.
- Provide supporting documentation with a note for each item showing how it connects to the position you are applying for.
- Tune your voice to a professional tone that shows energy and confidence but allows the evidence of professional training and experience to make your case.

INTERVIEW WITH A PUBLISHED WRITER: DANA ANDREW JENNINGS

Dana Jennings has published three novels: *Mosquito Games, Women of Granite,* and *Lonesome Standard Time,* and he is working on a fourth. He has also sold three picture books to Harcourt Brace. The first, *Me, Dad & No. 6,* was published in the spring of 1997. Jennings works full time as an editor on the sports desk of the *New York Times.* He started his newspaper career in New Hampshire as a reporter and later went on to work as an editor on the foreign desk of the *Wall Street Journal.* He also writes for the *New York Times,* mainly on culture and the arts. Dana Jennings's magazine essays and articles have appeared in *Esquire, Reader's Digest, New England Monthly, The Hudson Review,* and many other magazines that he says "you've never heard of."

Most interesting for this chapter, Dana Jennings spent five and a half years doing corporate communications for Dow Jones/The Wall Street Journal and CPC International, a Fortune 100 food company. He wrote and edited annual reports, press releases, and company publications.

What techniques do you use to make sure you have the information to revise a draft for a specific purpose? Do you outline or plan in any other way?

For a piece of journalism, I almost always end up gathering more material than I end up needing, and that makes revising easier. Let me explain: After I finish a first draft, I'll always see holes in the piece. Once the holes are identified, I go back to my notes and other information and hope that I have the story glue in there. We all know that we write with information, but we also rewrite with information.

Also, I always ask sources whether I can call them during the week when I'm completing a piece. It seems that a couple of questions always unexpectedly come up that only the source can answer; so, don't piss off your sources until you're sure a piece is done.

The way I set up a piece of journalism also lends itself to rewriting. Though a piece may appear seamless (I hope), each article is actually broken up into small parts that I approach one at a time. When I'm quickly writing a first draft, I'll note that certain parts need to be beefed up later on.

For fiction and essays, the process is different. The information I need to revise arises from constant rewriting, worrying, and dreaming. The information comes the way it magically comes onto the rice paper when one is doing a gravestone rubbing. It can't be rushed; it comes in its own time.

How do you anticipate the needs of your audience?

No matter what I write, from annual reports to newspaper articles to novels, I satisfy myself first. That's the only way I know how to write. Now, that isn't to say that I stiff the audience. In an annual report, I know going in what information the shareholders want to know about the company. In a newspaper article, I'll help the reader along through perhaps unfamiliar terrain. In my novels and essays . . . well, love it or leave it.

How do you know you need to revise a draft for a specific task?

Some pieces of writing have specific goals. The annual report lets shareholders know how the company is doing. The hard news story lets people know what's going on in their community. A press release puts the company's spin on a news event. When working at this kind of writing, the writer has to keep asking: Is this piece achieving its goal?

A couple of years ago I gave a commencement speech for lower-middle-class high school students graduating from a summer enrichment program. The bottom line for this speech was to make these kids feel good about themselves and their accomplishments, to let them know that others (namely me) had been where they had been and had gone on to succeed, and to send them on to their next steps with pride and hope. During the whole writing and rewriting process, I kept asking myself whether the piece was meeting those goals.

How do you distinguish rewriting from editing?

Sometimes, especially early on, rewriting and editing are the same thing. But, in the end, rewriting asks the big questions, while editing is just feather dusting. Rewriting covers finding holes in a piece, shaping it, ordering it, finding out whether you're really writing the right piece. A lot of students at the beginning of their writing careers confuse editing and rewriting. They think that a few fixed-up typos and some comma math (adding and subtracting—that game) add up to a rewrite. But real rewriting means firing up the Homelite, hauling out the Caterpillar, picking up the nine-pound hammer. Yeah, that John Henry was a rewriting man.

What attitudes do you find helpful as you revise?

I'm a born rewriter. Rewriting suits my soul. I'm a word doctor. I can tinker with a sentence, with a paragraph, the way my old man used to work on his race cars. I don't rush during rewriting. The hard part—the goddamned first draft—is done. Now I can explore the piece, whether it's a 700-word column or 75,000-word novel. Rewriting is the time to read your piece out loud, the time to challenge every verb and every noun. I rewrite the way an archaeologist approaches a buried city: with patience, and all the time trying to fill in the important missing gaps.

What specific process—or processes—do you use to revise a draft?

The best way to answer this question is to describe how I write. These days I write my first drafts longhand on Mead's Cambridge extrasmooth paper in a wirebound notebook. I write with Eberhard Faber's Design Ebony jet black extrasmooth pencils (number 6325); I love those pencils. This is how I write everything now, journalism and fiction. I rewrite and edit on the first draft: crossing out, inserting, making notes to myself. The usual mess. Then I take those handwritten pages and type them into my computer. I'm mainly keypunching here, but once in a while I'll make a change at this stage. Once the article or chapter is typed in, I print it out and attack it once again with my jet black extrasmooth pencil. Then I key in the changes, and print it out again. I NEVER REWRITE OR EDIT MY OWN WRITING ON THE COMPUTER. I like to take it slow, and the slowest way for me is at my desk, hunched over a piece of paper and scritch-scratching away.

Another key part of rewriting for me is reading any piece out loud. I write by ear. And I don't trust a piece of writing until I've heard it.

What different techniques do you use to respond to corporate writing tasks? How is your writing process different when you work on a newspaper story, an essay, a children's book, a novel?

Corporate writing: The most important thing to remember about corporate writing is this: It's their company, whoever *they* is. If you remember that, you won't go too crazy. As a corporate writer, I wrote annual and quarterly reports, wrote and edited the company newsletter and magazine, and wrote press releases. With all of these projects I used the skills I learned as a journalist. The main difference was that my sources were in house. And with each project, I wrote the best way I knew how and then let my superiors proceed to muck it up; writing for clarity isn't necessarily a plus in the corporate world.

Newspaper story: In the old days, when I was a daily newspaper reporter, I could bang it out with the best of them. Three or four stories a day, dictate a story over the phone, all that hard-news speed. I'm a lot slower now—because of my forays into essays and novel writing—and don't enjoy writing on a tight deadline. Even with a newspaper feature, I like to let it simmer, let the information steep in my head. Even as I'm gathering information, the story is percolating in my head. And I still write in drafts, not as many as for my creative writing, but I still work in drafts and rewrite a lot.

Personal essays, children's books, and novels: These are all of a piece, all brought up from the same well, share the same interior voice. The main difference is the gestation period. An essay can come together in a week, a children's picture book in a month, but a novel can take years. My first novel, *Mosquito Games,* came out in 1989, 10 years after I wrote the short story that grew into the novel.

But my basic technique is the same for these kinds of writing: working from an image (a woman sits alone at her kitchen table early one morning and is crying) or an observation (my 10-year-old son is now listening to his own music and rejecting my music), I start to brainstorm, writing as fast as I can what comes to me from these images and observations. I call this process "riffing," like some hot banjo player getting his solo in a bluegrass band. And the reason I do this so quickly is to get some energy, get some surprises. Once I get enough raw material, I'll slow down and start refining the raw ore.

Then what happens, what needs to happen, is that another image or observation jumps out of the pile and demands its own breakneck riff job. So, I'm still writing with information, like all good writers have to do, but the information is coming from the inside, not the outside.

What tools do you use to revise a draft?

As I said before, one of my major tools for revision is reading out loud. I trust my ear, and I need to hear my work read before I'm ready to be done with it. The ear knows when the head has screwed up.

Another important tool for revision is taking time off from a piece, if possible, even if it's only for a day. I find it hard to find holes in a piece when I'm in the heat of writing it. But if I can let the piece cool off, and then look at it a few days or a week later, it's easier for me to see broader flaws: information holes, rickety structure, wrong lead (don't you hate it when that happens?). With my novels, I'll often stop working two or three times in the course of the book and go back over what I've already written, taking notes as I go. As the book develops, I'll see holes that didn't exist before, I'll know that there is certain connective tissue that will have to be written, even whole chapters that I hadn't envisioned. Sometimes I'll even brainstorm off these chunks of the book.

On the micro level of rewriting, I obsess over my verbs and nouns, especially my verbs; I'm constantly looking for that infamous mot juste. And I think one of the strengths of my work is the vitality of its language. There isn't a verb in anything that I write that doesn't get challenged. And I'm not afraid to use the thesaurus and the dictionary; they help me remember what I already know. Some writers snobbishly say that they never use those tools; either their ready vocabulary is better than mine or they're prima donna fools.

How do you know when you've completed the process of revision?

There are two ways I know I'm done rewriting. The first is when the calendar on the wall says a piece is due; I refuse to blow a deadline.

The second is when the same comma keeps appearing and disappearing in the same sentence for about a week. That means it's time to hang it up and move on.

As a former editor at the **Wall Street Journal** *and as an editor on the* **New York Times** *sports desk, what are the most common writing problems you see, and how can they be solved?*

Before I talk about our writers' problems, first let me say that most of these journalists are working under fierce deadlines. Still, we are talking about the big leagues of journalism.

I still see too much use of the passive voice. These guys ought to know better. Attempts to make up for underreporting by overwriting. Treating an article as if it's a stand-up comedy routine where getting off a good line is more important than writing a good story; I'll admit that I'm guilty of this sometimes, too, when I write—I'm kind of a wise guy. A lot of my colleagues don't know how to write a good feature. Most of them think a feature is a story with a snappy lead followed by a string of quotes. They don't have a clue about how anecdotes move a story along (I count the number of anecdotes I have in one of my own pieces to make sure there are enough). They don't understand the use of the telling detail or the selective use of quotes. I would say that most of the feature stories in the *New York Times* sports section fail.

If a writer needs to revise, what is the most helpful way to deliver that news? What is the most effective way for your editors to tell you that you need to revise?

The relationship between writer and editor on a newspaper is a tricky thing. Many writers don't like the copydesk, and believe that our only purpose is to screw up their copy. Then again, the columnist George Vecsey, who is possibly our best writer, won an award last year and thanked the copydesk for the times it saved his ass.

Being the editor: It's always best to tell the writer what works in a piece first before moving on to the negative. An editor shouldn't be dictator. The best approach for me is to act as a coach and a colleague who wants the piece to be as good as it can be. I don't give orders, I make suggestions. And suggestions are always easier for a writer to take. "Why don't we make the 10th graf the lead?" goes down a lot better than "This lead sucks; the real lead is buried in the story."

Being the writer: Basically, I want to be treated as a writer the way I treat writers as an editor. All of us need good editors. In journalism, the one thing I object to is when an editor tries to force a preconceived notion into one of my pieces. And this happens a fair amount at the *Times.* Everyone is smart, and some editors think they know your story better than you do.

The best editor I've worked with is my children's book editor, Liz Van Doren at Harcourt Brace. I had never tried writing children's books before I hooked up with Liz, and during the past five years she has patiently taught me what writing for 4- to 8-year-olds is all about. She is always forthright about a manuscript and treats each one seriously. She is also as patient as I am stubborn. She recently bought a picture-book manuscript from me called *Leaf Dragon.* That book, which I first showed to Liz in 1991, has gone through at least 10 real rewrites in the past five years, not to mention my own intermediate rewrites. But, together, we made it work.

What are the most important three things you've learned as a publishing writer that you wish you had known when you went to college?

I've learned that hard work and perseverance matter a lot more than raw talent. When I was in college, I thought that talent counted for a lot. But when I look at the ranks of professional writers, I see a lot more honorable pluggers than incendiary geniuses. I've learned to work hard, but when I was younger I wished I had worked harder.

Having a novel published (or articles printed in the *New York Times*) doesn't change your life. The actual writing may change your life (certainly with a novel) but not publication. I'm still just a hick from small-town New Hampshire trying to get some words down every day. And some days are better than others. The writing is love, publication is just one (big, but ephemeral) orgasm.

The older you get, the less you know—and that's a healthy thing. I was easy to please in 1976, when I first started writing for *The New Hampshire*, perfection wasn't so far off. Today, I happily feel like old Hokusai as perfection recedes even as my work improves.

I may use a test reader but I instruct that reader: "I know I have to do more research, but is the order of the information right for you?" "I think the order's right but what about the voice?" "Would this report persuade you to support me?" I do not return to a test reader who does not make me want to write when I leave.

When someone rejects the report, I listen to what they are saying, go out and bark at stray dogs, then figure out how to solve the problem. The customer may not always be right, but you had better act as if he or she is. Your job is to deliver information in such a way that it will achieve a specific decision. The report reader holds all the cards.

COMMENTARY

The new communication technology increases the need for people who master the writer's craft. Technology shrinks our world and people in Tokyo and Tennessee, Prague and Philadelphia, Rio and Edinburgh, and Beijing and Nairobi need to share ideas, policies, and products. They are shared by people who write and rewrite until meaning comes clear across the barriers of distance and culture. Entrepreneur and scholar, radical and conservative, doctor and research scientist, soldier and pacifist, manufacturer and environmentalist all have to speak a language each can understand. That language is built from messages understood and misunderstood, written and rewritten between people who discover they have become dependent on each other in our shrinking world.

CHAPTER 10

THE CRAFT OF
LETTING GO

The beginning writer may resist at first, but once introduced to revision and its rewards of discovery and craft, rewriting can become addictive. Writers brag that they have written three drafts, nine, a dozen, even more. In a famous *Paris Review* interview Ernest Hemingway said, "I rewrote the ending to *Farewell to Arms,* the last page of it, 39 times before I was satisfied." George Plimpton asked, "Was there some technical problem there? What was it that had you stumped?" Hemingway answered, "Getting the words right."

Some writers never stop getting the words right. They keep fiddling with manuscripts that never get published because they are never submitted. If I ever end up in a mental institution it may be because I am starting a book and cannot get beyond the decision to begin with "A" or "The"—or was it "The" or "A"? Close attention to the writer's craft is important, but it can easily become obsessive. A beginning writer I knew kept revising the first few pages of his book day after day, week after week. I taped a cardboard box so it could not be opened, cut a slot in the top, and then gave it to him. At the end of each day he put the day's pages in the box so he could not go back to them until the next morning. He had to move on to write new pages. He wrote the book and it became very influential in its field.

....

WHY WRITERS DON'T LET GO

Most of us have good reasons for keeping our drafts stored in memory. There is a secret delight in examining them in the privacy of our computer room. Alone, we can bring up the draft, mark where more research will help, draft a new order, move a section up earlier or back later, repack a paragraph, connect two sentences or cut a long one in two, sharpen a phrase, activate a verb, pick a nicer typeface, run the spell check, zap the draft back into memory.

FEAR OF EXPOSURE

We act as though sending a manuscript out and getting it published will reveal ourselves—and it will. What we write reveals how we think and feel. The information we collect and value, the way we order it into meaning, the music or voice we use to share it with a reader exposes both our brain and our heart.

But so does silence. If we do not speak we are heard as a person who is not involved, who neither thinks nor feels. Writing and publishing is nothing more than an act of living. When we think and care and share our thoughts and our feelings, we are participating in the remaking of the world, nothing less. We need to develop the courage to reveal ourselves and it does take courage. As a teacher I often found that those who had the most to say were most reluctant to say it.

OBSESSION WITH CORRECTNESS

The best students not only care about their subject matter, they care about their craft. These students want to write right. They have a fear of error and at school, home, and work they had been marked down or even ridiculed because they made a mistake in usage, mechanics, or spelling. Often the person who was most critical was wrong— "You have to start with a topic sentence" [Wrong]; "You can't use a sentence fragment" [Wrong]; "You can't use a contraction" [Wrong]; "You can't start a sentence with *but* or *and*" [Wrong]; "A paragraph must have five sentences" [Wrong]—but they sound as if they know what they are saying. And who wants to get yelled at? Better not to make yourself vulnerable.

It is good to clean up the final draft—run the spell check, make sure the punctuation only breaks tradition for good reason, print out a clean copy free of typographical errors—but the writer must realize that each publisher or editor or teacher has individual rules that contradict each other and can not be anticipated. I do a weekly column, but I have different editors with different rules on the copydesk; I write books for different publishers who, in turn, hire different copyeditors. I must make my writing as clear as I can; I must break the traditions of writing only if it is necessary to make my evolving meaning clear. Then, I have to submit my drafts.

CONTINUING DISCOVERY

It is easier for me to battle my obsession with error than to stop the process of discovery that goes on with each draft. I do not so much write to produce a problem-free draft as I write to explore my world. I come to the desk tired of the subject, ready—even eager—to let it go and start tinkering with a line or a paragraph, and I catch something in the draft in the corner of my eye that needs exploration. For example, I am describing my dysfunctional childhood and spot an idea new to me: I was more comfortable than many soldiers with the surrealistic confusion of combat because I was familiar with the surrealistic confusion of my home. I want to include that in what I am writing when I should put it aside. It is worth a new poem, an essay, a chapter in the novel I am writing.

Most of us become obsessive, compulsive, never-let-go rewriters because of the excitement and satisfaction of revision. We do not as often learn how little we know as how much we know. The act of revision ignites memory, connects information that we had never connected until we begin to rewrite. We could go on, revising this draft for a week, a month, a year, and some writers—or nonwriters—have gone on revising for a lifetime.

·····

HOW TO LET GO

We have to teach ourselves to let go, to deliver the term paper or the scientific paper or the memo or the critical essay or the story or the research paper or the poem or the grant proposal or the screenplay or the case history. The piece of writing that remains in the computer is wasted.

DEADLINES

The most effective way to let go is to establish a deadline and meet it. I write my columns a week ahead, on Monday morning before lunch, and I love lunch. My poems are written by the second or fourth Thursday of each month when my poetry group meets. I am finishing this book on the Sunday before Election Day, my deadline. Tomorrow I will establish a deadline for finishing the draft of my novel. Once I have that deadline I will march backward through the calendar establishing weekly deadlines and breaking them into daily deadlines. I will not go as far as the famous Victorian novelist Anthony Trollope who worked as postal inspector and wrote on the road between inspections or even when he was on vacation:

> As I journeyed across France and Marseilles, and made thence a terribly rough voyage to Alexandria, I wrote my allotted number of pages every day. On this occasion more than once I left my paper on the cabin table, rushing away to be sick in the privacy of my stateroom. It was February, and the weather was miserable; but still I did my work.
>
> It has . . . become my custom . . . to write with my watch before me, and to require from myself 250 words every quarter of an hour. I have found that the 250 words have been forthcoming as regularly as my watch went.
>
> There are those who would be ashamed to subject themselves to such a taskmaster, and who think that the man who works with his imagination should allow himself to wait till inspiration moves him. . . . To me it would not be more absurd if the shoemaker were to wait for inspiration, or the tallow-chandler for the divine moment of melting. . . .

The daily deadline—externally or self-imposed—is the best way of letting go.

COLLABORATION

Another reason to let go is to collaborate with a fellow writer, a classmate, a colleague, a teacher, an editor who can help you see what needs to be done and how it may be accomplished. I was struggling with Chapter 9 of this book and could have gone on trying this, trying that, but I knew I needed fresh eyes. I sent the chapter off to Laurie Runion, an editor I have collaborated with—and always learned from—in the past, feeling the chapter was not as good as I wanted it to be. She came up with the idea of case histories to demonstrate some of the tasks writers are assigned in the workplace—and I followed through on it.

I have cultivated a community of writers to whom I can send a draft that does not yet seem right. Sometimes they even tell me revision is not necessary, but most times I learn what needs to be done, do it, then let the manuscript go.

DECREASED DISCOVERY

The most aesthetic reason is the most rare for me. That is when you see little possibility in the draft. There is no discovery, no learning, no excitement. If that happens, let it go. It deserves a life of its own.

WHEN YOU LET GO

Writing is an act of communication. Of course, that communication early on is between writer and draft, but as the draft gets its own legs under itself, hears its own voice, it needs to go off on its own.

READERS MAKE THE DRAFT THEIRS

Letting drafts go is like letting children go. It is hard to, but they return—most of the time—as adults and friends. They have changed, and you can delight in their difference and their similarity. We do not own our children and we do not own our drafts. In a column, I wrote about the experience of meeting my readers:

> As long as I have written, I am still surprised by the intimate and individual relationship I have with each reader.
>
> We meet in the privacy of each other's minds and then, on occasion, we meet in the flesh and are suddenly strangers, not quite the people we were when one of us wrote alone and the other read alone.

A short time ago I met many of my readers at one time as Minnie Mae and I sat in the *Globe* booth at CVS Senior Expo in Boston.

It was a wonderful and disconcerting experience. I have grown relatively comfortable with my neighbors who read the column, although often startled when they start talking.

I have usually written the column they have read a week or more before, have written another column or two since, and am rehearsing the one I will write next. The reader, fresh from the column they have read, must wonder at my confusion as I try to pick up the thread of the private conversation the reader had with me when I was on the page.

I am often flattered but startled at what they have read in my piece. They have not read the column I wrote but an essay that has been written in their mind as their autobiography changes my text.

Write to communicate, we say in class and that was, in fact, the title of an elementary school writing program I wrote that has long been out of print. But what we communicate is not what we intend—at least not in fiction, poetry, or the personal essay.

I was disconcerted by that when I was first published, but I soon came to realize that was the magic of writing. Nothing I wrote was read as I expected. Readers with their own experiences, feelings, needs came to my published draft, and when things went well we shared in the creation of a draft that was neither mine nor theirs, but ours.

And then we meet in the supermarket, on the sidewalk or parking lot, at Ron's, The Bagelry, or Pine Garden. We know each other so well. We have written a text that helps us battle the fear of aging, survive the death of a child, or makes us laugh at the fact that young people are behaving, God forbid, as we did when we were young.

But the column was written in the privacy of my office, often when my shoes—and sometimes a good deal more—were off, and then was read by a reader in nightclothes at the kitchen table, in bed, or even in what we call the reading room.

When we create this draft, we speak to each other, perhaps more intimately than we have spoken to those close to us or even to ourselves.

Amazed at what we have said in private, we do not know what to say in public, and so readers praise us, telling us how wonderfully we write and we preen and shuffle in what may appear to be false modesty.

It is not modesty at all. What makes me uncomfortable when I am praised for what I have written is that each of us has collaborated on these drafts.

I write and it is only ink on paper. It comes alive when a reader smiles, nods, sheds a tear, seeing, feeling, thinking what I cannot know. The draft has become, as it should, the reader's draft.

I write of my daughter and a reader sees a son long gone; I write of Minnie Mae and a reader sees Ralph with whom she shares the sometimes terrifying, sometimes hilarious experience of growing old; I write of infantry war in Europe and he sees naval warfare in the Pacific.

And so when we meet away from the page and shake hands and a reader tells me he or she likes my column, I smile and mumble appreciation but want to say what I am saying now.

It is our column. The magic is that each Tuesday I write the column I need to write—to stare down my ghosts, to accept, to relive, to mourn, to understand, to rage, to laugh, and then you, the reader, bring your life to my page.

We write a column together, sharing a personal moment when we remember, think, feel together. It is not a column I have written, but what we have written in collaboration that is my wonder and my delight. Thank you for what we have written together at the kitchen table or in the reading room.

Let your writing go and you will be in touch with readers who will take your writing and make it their own. You will be playing a role in the human community, having your say.

FREE TO WRITE

When you let go of your draft you are free to write again, to do as my closest writing friend, Chip Scanlan, says, "To do the writing only you can do." We need to know what you have discovered you know by writing and rewriting and revising and editing and, at the end, by letting go.

INDEX